C000140133

Memories
of
Gloucester

Part of the
Memories
series

Memories
of
Gloucester

*The Publishers would like to thank the following companies for supporting
the production of this book*

Bennetts Coaches

Dancey + Meredith Architects

Fielding & Platt International Limited

Gloucester Antiques Centre Limited

Gloucester Charities Trust

Gloucester City Markets

Halls & Keck

Hamilton House Group

LVS (Gloucester) Limited

Marshall Langston Limited

Pressweld Limited

First published in Great Britain by True North Books Limited
Units 3 - 5 Heathfield Industrial Park
Elland West Yorkshire
HX5 9AE
Tel. 01422 377977
© Copyright: True North Books Limited 2000

All rights reserved. No part of this publication may be reproduced, stored in a retrieval system, or transmitted in any
form, or by any means, electronic, mechanical, photocopy, recording or otherwise without the prior permission in
writing of the Copyright holders, nor be otherwise circulated in any form or binding or cover other than in which it is
published and without a similar condition being imposed on the subsequent publisher.

ISBN 1 903204 04 6

*Text, design and origination by True North Books Limited
Printed and bound by The Amadeus Press Limited*

Introduction from The Citizen

For 2,000 years Gloucester has played a prominent part in English history and during these two millennia the city has had the rare distinction of having been continuously lived in. Originally its strategic importance as the lowest crossing point of the Severn was recognised by the Romans who later established a colonia here for retired officers - one of only four in the country.

During the 'Dark Ages' the Saxons laid out the existing city street pattern and evidence of their stay can still be seen at St Oswald's Priory. Following the Norman conquest William the Conqueror ordered the Domesday survey while holding court in Gloucester. In 1216 King Henry III was crowned in the city's St Peter's Abbey and just over a century later the murdered Edward II was laid to rest there - which ironically sparked a tourist boom as pilgrims flocked to the King's tomb.

In 1470 the City played a decisive role in the Wars of the Roses when it refused entry and passage to a Lancastrian force which then marched north to Tewkesbury where it was discovered and routed by Yorkists under Edward lV.

In the Tudor period the saintly but luckless Bishop John Hooper was martyred within sight of his cathedral, while during the English Civil War in 1643, the Parliamentarians within the city withstood a siege which almost certainly altered the course of the war and subsequent English history.

It was here that one of the most magnificent cathedrals in the world was built. Gloucester is also one of the homes of the world's oldest music festival - the Three Choirs. The Sunday School movement began here and the great 18th century evangelist George Whitefield who is revered on both sides of the Atlantic was born in Gloucester

In more recent centuries, Gloucester's industries have flourished with its products being exported all over the world. Typical of these was the Gloucester Railway Carriage and Wagon Company which produced rolling stock not only for Britain's railways but also built up a massive export trade as well.

It was on the edge of the city too that the Gloster Aircraft Company pioneered some of the greatest aviation achievements of the last century. GAC produced a succession of successful military aircraft, set world records and in Britain's 'darkest hour' produced thousands of front line aircraft during the second world war. It was also a Gloster plane which first demonstrated the potential of jet flight and, when produced as the Gloster Meteor, took aviation into a new era.

Since 1722, first the Gloucester Journal and, since 1876, The Citizen has charted the city's history. The newspapers' reporters and photographers have recorded the city's continuing development as its boundaries have been extended, its population has boomed, its industrial base has been transformed from heavy engineering to high-tec and its docks have evolved from a thriving port importing and exporting goods worldwide into one of the region's top tourist attractions. The newspaper's archives are a rich source of historical material some of which is reproduced here. With the help of its readers The Citizen has also produced a series of Bygone Gloucestershire supplements which has served to remind Gloucestrians of their proud and distinguished past.

The Citizen

Contents

Events & *occasions*

An old tradition is seen here coming to an end: Gloucester Market was on the verge of moving from its old spot in the city centre to its new spot out on St Oswald's Road at the time of this photograph, leaving its old spot free to become, in due course, a bus station and shops. It would be nice to report that the last lot sold before the move was a pen of Gloucester Old Spots - lovely pigs, and very tasty, but a designated Rare Breed; so it was a far more typical sale, that of a pen of Large White crossbred pigs, which brought to an end livestock dealing at the city centre site. The occasion did not go unmarked: speeches were made, and the auctioneers presented inscribed tankards to both the buyer and the seller of the pigs. Wielding the hammer as the last lot was sold was Mr Cecil Bruton, whose great-grandfather had conducted his first sale on that very spot almost a century ago in 1862. Names such as Bruton Knowles, Pearce Pope and J Pearce Pope & Sons have long been associated in the area with auctions, and the city has a strong auctioneering tradition, with Gloucester contestants frequently being selected to represent the Somerset & Gloucestershire branch of the Incorporated Society of Auctioneers in the annual competition, and enjoying great success.

This page and overleaf: There was widespread discontent throughout Britain at the government's economic policy in the late 1950s. The 1958 Trades Union Congress at Bournemouth condemned the government's inability to maintain full employment, and also criticised its use of the bank rate to control inflation. Some arguments seem destined to roll on down the centuries . . . However, Gloucester had specific cause for worry in October 1958. Unemployment in the city stood at around one thousand, and two major local employers, Rotol Limited at Staverton and Armstrong Siddeley

(Brockworth) Ltd, were both warning of impending redundancies. So the two factories decided to stage a joint redundancy march on Tuesday 7th October, setting off from their respective factories just before 'knocking-off time'. It rained, but that did not deter the men; hundreds of factory workers took part in the demonstration. The two marches converged at Wotton Pitch, where the road from Brockworth meets the Cheltenham road; in one of our photographs the side of the Fleece Hotel is visible behind the group of demonstrators who are pushing their bicycles.

Continued from previous page: From here, the men proceeded in a united procession to the Guildhall, where they presented their petitions to the Mayor. The slogans on the demonstrators' banners vary considerably in tone, but the message is the same. There is the direct approach: 'We want work', 'The AEU fights for the right to work', and 'Work is a right, not a privilege'. Then there is the sarcastic approach: 'Vote Tory for full unemployment', and '4,000 redundant - You have never had it better'. And then there was the cryptic approach: 'Turn your swords into plough shares', 'This is our life', and 'Are we being sent to Coventry?' - this last being a reference to Armstrong Siddeley's announcement that it was transferring production of its aero engines to its Coventry plant. Last but not least there was the artistic approach, which appears to show a carrot labelled 'work' and a donkey labelled 'Tory government', along with the slogan 'Are we flogging a dead horse'; no doubt it all made perfect sense to the marchers. Overall, however, it was made abundantly clear what the men's demands were. There was no violence, although many of the men must have been dreadfully worried by the prospect of losing their jobs - and their worst fears were confirmed a mere couple of weeks later when it was announced that the Armstrong Siddeley factory was to close. Negotiations were going on behind the scenes at Rotol as well, but in this case the outcome was somewhat more encouraging; by 1960 the factory had become part of the Dowty Group, and the company went on to enjoy prosperity by securing some very good contracts.

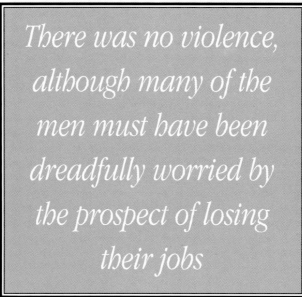

> *There was no violence, although many of the men must have been dreadfully worried by the prospect of losing their jobs*

The skimpy nightie has certainly brought a collective grin to the audience's face; but how many of the ladies present rushed out to buy one after the show, we wonder? Fashion Shows have long been recognised in the Gloucester area as a thoroughly enjoyable entertainment and a good way of raising funds. The golden jubilee celebrations of the County branch of the National Farmers' Union in 1959 included a memorable fashion show put on for the farmers' wives, but our photograph show an earlier event held at Wesley Church, Cinderford (about 15 miles west of Gloucester), in November 1958. As well as the nightwear seen here, a wide variety of. daywear and beachwear was displayed by professional models alongside local young people. During the 20th century supermodels like Twiggy brought a new kind of high-profile glamour to the modelling profession - together with a new and perhaps not altogether healthy obsession with slimming; while the designer-label ethos introduced a cut-throat, competitive edge into the fashion business, and annual lingerie shows became important events on the international fashion world's calendar. But the professional models who went along to Cinderford were perfectly happy to pass on a few catwalk tips to the amateurs, and the show was a very friendly and enjoyable occasion, which swelled church funds nicely. Not surprisingly, the local girls voted unanimously to leave the bed-time attire up to the professionals in order to avoid embarrassment. The model padding demurely down the aisle in a frilly nightdress must have found the floorboards a little cold on her bare feet!

Below: Contrary to appearances, these visitors have not travelled by boat all the way from Nigeria to Gloucester Shipyard; they have in fact come to Britain on a goodwill tour sponsored by the Central Office of Information. Looking back from a 21st century standpoint, it might come as something of a shock to realise that it is only as recently as the second half of the last century that Africa became independent from British colonial rule. Perhaps more surprising still is the fact that Nigeria received its first ever visit from a serving British Prime Minister when Harold Macmillan went there as part of his African tour in 1960. African nationalism was growing, and Britain recognised that there were 'winds of change blowing through Africa'. On 1st October 1963 Nigeria became a Republic within the British Commonwealth, and the two countries began adjust to their new relationship with each other,

perhaps seeing one another in a new light. So the Central Office of Information organised a tour to help the Nigerian delegation get to know the people of Britain - and where better to send the three Nigerian trade unionists than Gloucester! When the photographer caught up with them, the group was engrossed in observing the tanker Wheeldale undergoing repairs in the dry dock, and no doubt Mr A D Nhexi (standing underneath the letter Y) took a professional interest in the goings on, as he held the post of Deputy General Secretary of the Nigerian Ports Authority.

Bottom: Looking at this photograph, it is hard to decide which will present the most unfamiliar sight to a modern reader - a herd of circus elephants, or an unpaved Eastgate Street with the Cadena Cafe and Hardy's. In the mid-1960s, Hardy's and the Cadena Cafe were as much a part of Gloucester as the Guildhall - but a herd of elephants was clearly something of a novelty. What it means, of course, is that Billy Smart's Circus is in town; the 15 elephants have just got off the train and, after freshening up after their journey, are on their way to Oxleaze where the Big Top has been erected. Other circus performers will include the monkeys, the horses, the camel, and some humans as well - the latter group including acrobats, clowns and flying trapeze artistes. There is something for everyone at a circus. Little girls love the glamour of the costumes and dream of riding round the ring on the galloping horses, while little boys are more impressed by the antics of the acrobats on the high-wire or the skill and courage of the animal trainers. In more recent years, circuses and their treatment of animals have come under close scrutiny, and some circuses no longer include animal acts; but in the 1960s, a Big Top without animals would have been unthinkable.

Below: Do any readers remember going to one of the Civic Christmas Parties at the Guildhall? And being served by the Mayor and Mayoress? Here, it is Councillor and Mrs Bennett who are doing the honours; but while normally children would be intrigued by the mayor's chain, it is doubtful if they have even noticed it this time - not when there are buns to be had. Children don't change much over the years - though as we can see from this photograph, their clothes do. To begin with, how many boys would wear ties for a children's party in the 21st century? It is noticeable, too, how many pairs of knees are visible. Little boys generally wore shorts until they went to secondary school; as often as not a boy's first pair of trousers came as part of his new school uniform, and suddenly, he looked very grown-up. Not until the last generation or so have small children been dressed like miniature adults. Little girls had frocks, little boys had shorts, and as often as not children's clothes were handed down and passed around until they finally fell apart at the seams, with no small voices raised to complain that all their friends have the latest designer gear and why can't they?

Right: Gloucester Carnival has been the big event of the summer for as long as any of us can remember, and the 1958 Carnival was a glorious affair. It began with a mile-long procession which drew one of the biggest carnival crowds ever; the colourful tableaux were, as always, varied and inventive, and the winning tableau on this occasion was a particularly novel one, on a very topical theme. During 1958 the litter laws had been changed, making it possible for members of the public to bring a prosecution against anyone whom they saw dropping litter; so the Gloucester Corporation Highways Department took the opportunity of hammering home the message in a light-hearted way by transforming themselves into Litter Rats. They made such appealing little rodents that, far from offending anyone, they actually won first prize. Here, however, it is the Fancy Dress prize which is being hotly contested, and again one of the competitor's imaginations has been inspired by the Keep Britain Tidy theme, but a baby doll seems to be carrying off the prize. Judging the fancy dress is an unenviable task, but although competitors might be a little disappointed not to win anything, they have had all the fun of making their costume, getting dressed up and taking part in the parade. Presenting the prizes here is Councillor Mrs Langdon, watched by the Mayor and an immense crowd of smiling spectators.

A banner on the back of this carnival float reminds us that it is the 25th anniversary of Battle of Britain Week, and in the background is the War Memorial in Parkend Road; so the few to whom we all owe so much are not forgotten as Gloucester enjoys what many termed its biggest and best Carnival parade ever. The marvellous Minstrel tableau seen here was put on by members of the RAFA Ladies' Committee; elsewhere in the parade were a horde of Zulu warriors, alias the staff of Airtight Aluminium Windows, and Bon Marche's desert tableau with a camel pulling a gigantic Sphinx, created over two months using some 400 yards of red and gold foil. Topical tableaux reflecting 60s influences included a pirate radio ship (Radio Caroline and Radio Luxembourg were upsetting the GPO at the time by using up an airwave or two to transmit pop music and commercials to a wide audience who loved their style of broadcasting); the gaol break of Great Train Robber Ron Biggs, whose meticulously-planned escape from Winson Green Prison, Birmingham, hit the headlines; and the Daleks, who inspired the tableau which brought Sharpness Boys Club first prize for Best Tableau by a Youth Organisation.

Right: May was traditionally a month of parades; the end of winter meant that people could once again take to the streets with a reasonable chance of not getting wet - although the large umbrella by the District Bank shows that this was not always the case - and organisations became active again. The annual parade of the Commonwealth Youth Service, as it used to be called, was one of the spectacles which regularly drew large crowds of spectators, and the air would ring to the sound of drums and trumpets as groups including the Air Cadets, the Sea Cadets, the Army Cadets, the Boy Scouts, the Girl Guides and the Boys Brigade marched through the city streets. On our photograph we see the Boy Scouts parading along Eastgate Street, to arrive in due course at the Cathedral for a special service. The Gloucester Scouts would already have held their annual 'Bob-a-Job' week, so thanks to their efforts the citizens of Gloucester would have tidy gardens, clean cars and everything in apple-pie order, and the coffers of the organisation would be that much the richer. Their achievements were impressive; during 1965's Bob-a-Job week, for instance, they topped the previous year's total by £200 to raise a record-breaking £1,357.19s.8d (£1,357.98p) - from which we deduce that either someone lost fourpence, or people did not always pay in complete 'bobs' (a 'bob' being a shilling, or 12d - in modern currency, 5p).

Below: There is something irresistible about the rousing music of a military band. No matter how many marching bands you've seen before and no matter how busy you are, it is hard to resist the temptation to stop what you're doing and watch the parade go past. In this case the band in question is the Band of the Royal Corps of Signal, with their bright red tunics and blue trousers turning Westgate Street into a blaze of colour, and their trumpets and drums filling the air with sound. They are in fact on their way to the park, where the music will continue. Concerts in the park always attract a good crowd, and on this occasion the audience will hear a good variety of tunes, both old favourites and more up-to-date numbers. The afternoon's programme will include music by Handel and John Philip Souza, The Planemakers, and the theme from Z-Cars, the popular TV series launched by the BBC in 1962. Many viewers followed the fortunes of the Newtown police eagerly each week as they patrolled their fictional area of Liverpool in their Ford Zephyrs; one of the serial's great strengths was its well-drawn characters, with leading roles taken by actors Jeremy Kemp, James Ellis, Colin Welland and Brian Blessed - who apparently could not drive.

Above: Two decades after the end of the second world war, the crowds who have gathered to see the Glorious Glosters pass by on this warm summer's day can be divided into those who experienced the war, and those who didn't. Of course the post-war generation has sat on its parents' knees and listened to tales of the wartime, and studied the events of 1939-1945 in history, but only those who lived through those years really know what wartime Britain was like - the sounds, the atmosphere, and the little details of everyday life. To many of the older generation, the stirring sight of soldiers and tanks parading through the streets of Gloucester may have brought back memories of loved ones killed in action. But to the youngsters the parade is above all glamorous and exciting - at least, that is what the recruiting sergeant is hoping; this display is in fact the climax of a recruiting campaign. In the 1960s National Service was no longer obligatory, so it was now up to the Armed Forces to promote themselves in order to attract new recruits. No doubt many a schoolboy stood open-mouthed, watching the Mayor, Councillor Mrs D Embling, taking the salute outside the Guildhall with the City High Sheriff and the Colonel of the Regiment, and resolved that one day, when he was a few years older, he would be one of the 200 men on parade.

Below: It must be a varied life, being a Queen. Within the space of a few weeks Her Majesty was to be seen in her official capacity, stepping across a red carpet at Victoria Station, dressed in a frock and coat of silver grey with a heavy stole collar and a small matching hat, to welcome the Shah of Persia to Britain - and in a less official capacity, striding out from Badminton House towards the ring at the Badminton Horse Trials, on a path laid with straw, wearing wellies and a sensible coat and carrying her own brolly. The smile on her face says quite clearly that she is glad to be here, and is not just putting in a dutiful appearance; and indeed Gloucester folk who are regular participants or visitors at Badminton will know that the Queen is never put off by mud and rain. The year of our photograph is 1959, and this was a memorably wet year; the ground was so completely sodden that most of the thousand or so vehicles parked by visitors got stuck in the mud and had to be hauled out by farm tractors. The Queen's white Rolls Royce was not among the vehicles that suffered this embarrassment, but the BBC Television outside broadcast truck was, and it had to be got out of the field at the end of the day by a caterpillar tractor.

On the move

Those elegant badges on this hut leave us wondering why in later years the AA opted to give its members very plain, square badges. This is the Automobile Association Patrol Service Centre at Highnam. In fact it was situated at the junction of the A48 to South Wales and the A40 to Ross, installed in time to assist members who ran into difficulties over the May bank holiday, 1959. The radio aerial on the roof gives us an indication of just how technologically advanced the rescue service was; the AA was extremely proud of its two-way radio system, which had a range of ten miles. A team of four patrols manned the control centre, with one inside by the radio, one outside ostensibly to deal with members' problems but perhaps also briefed to enrol new members, and two very, very nice men out on the road. Many readers will remember the days when AA membership brought with it an envelope containing a large key which would unlock any of the AA emergency telephone boxes up and down the country. Fewer readers will ever have used their key, however, because AA boxes had become so few and far between that your chances of ever breaking down outside one of them were pretty remote.

*A*ny 21st century Jaguar fan whose prized Mk II saloon had just had a close encounter with a bus would be very hard put to smile; but the hapless owner of this crumpled vehicle at least had the consolation of knowing that when his insurance paid out, he should be able to get a replacement. If he did, let us hope he was a little more careful with it; in subsequent years the Mk II Jaguar, powered by the famous XK engine, became highly collectible, and by the end of the 20th century a classic Mk II in good condition was worth a small fortune. Even when Jaguar's classic models were in full production they were not always easy to obtain; during the post-war years Britain's manufacturers were pressed to export as much as they could, and

Jaguar was so successful in obtaining orders from America that the factory was working to full capacity just to meet export orders. Although Britain's motor industry was not without its troubles during the second half of the 20th century, the Jaguar name and reputation has stood the test of time and continues to symbolise the very best of British values. Television viewers will agree that Inspector Morse, that well-respected Oxford gentleman, just wouldn't be the same without his immaculately-preserved Mk II. We strongly suspect, however, that restoration and preservation was not an option for this particular car, which judging from appearances is unlikely to have recovered from its unfortunate mishap at the junction of Hatheley Road and Tredworth Road.

Below: A couple of recent developments at the end of Westgate Street were recorded by this photographer in the summer of 1959. For a start, the traffic island at the junction with the Gloucester ring road represents a brand new challenge for Gloucester's motorists; fortunately they will have time to get used to it before the worst of the summer traffic to and from South Wales begins. Before the ring road was completed the city had to brace itself for traffic chaos every summer, which grew worse each year as the number of cars on the roads increased. The idea of the island is to separate ring road traffic, which will pass to the left, from city traffic which will pass to the right. And, to continue the theme of cars, Healey's garage in the background is still relatively new on the scene itself, having been opened the previous October. As Morris dealers they can look forward to a prosperous decade. In fact Morris Motors had already merged with Austin to form BMC in 1952; this group later become part of British Leyland, and the Morris name was eventually swallowed up. But before this famous British marque finally disappeared, a number of memorable models bearing the Morris badge went on to enjoy great popularity during the 60s,

including the Morris Minor which in 1961 became the first British car to reach a production figure of a million, the stately Morris Oxford, the ubiquitous Morris 1100, and of course the legendary Mini-Minor.

Bottom: It may look a chaotic scene, but it was actually a well-thought-out exercise in preventing traffic chaos and as such was succeeding very well. Before the construction of the relief road Gloucester's worst traffic nightmares always occurred in the summer, when the holiday traffic from the South Wales and the Ross roads descended en masse upon the city and caused everything to grind to a halt. August bank holiday was the worst time of all, and local motorists always dreaded it; but on this particular bank holiday weekend Gloucester was determined that for once it would not grind to a halt. So it divided the traffic coming over Westgate Bridge into two lanes; traffic going into the city centre took the right-hand lane, leaving the left-hand lane for the through traffic which could then filter left into St Oswald's Road without being held up by those waiting to go straight ahead. A policeman was put on point duty to stop the traffic along St

Oswald's road and let the city-bound traffic across at regular intervals. To the 21st century motorist, accustomed to sophisticated traffic systems, it seems a simple enough idea; however, at the time it seemed quite a radical step to take. Unfortunately it still did not help drivers who were trying to get out of Gloucester, and during Saturday afternoon a queue of cars still built up right back to the Cross.

Both pages: Nobody who used to commute into Gloucester regularly will ever forget Barton Gates; the scenes pictured here will be etched on the memory of many a motorist. The advertising hoardings along this particular stretch of Barton Street - on this photograph we can see one poster informing us that 'Regent stations serve you well', and further along an advert for Ideal Milk - must have been some of Gloucester's prime advertising sites, as they had a captive audience of queues of travellers looking round for something to occupy their thoughts for as long as the gates were closed! With around fifty trains a day passing the spot, the chances of having to wait were quite high. Worst of all was when you saw the stop signal come on just as you were approaching; this meant that you were in for a four or five minute delay. The sequence of events which followed became very familiar. First you would watch the man come and close the gates. Their operation was synchronised so that when he swung one of the main gates either open or closed, the whole set, consisting of four main gates and four wicket gates, would also open or close. The gatekeeper's next task was to place two wooden struts against the gates to keep them safely closed until he had returned to his cabin to raise the lever which raised the metal stop blocks. Then everybody sat and waited for the train. Finally you would be rewarded by the crescendoing sound of steam, followed by the climactic moment when the train passed; and a brief, tense pause: would you now be able to continue your journey, or was it one of those occasions when the gates stayed shut in anticipation of another train a few minutes later? With a bit of luck the metal blocks would clank back down, the gatekeeper would emerge and the gate-opening sequence would begin. It was no good getting impatient; Barton Gates were a fact of life, and though we may have cursed them under out breath at the time, now they are gone, some of us feel nostalgic for them - or, at least, for the days when the motor vehicle was not the undisputed king of transport.

This photograph will make many readers nostalgic for the days of steam - leaning out of the window and getting smuts in your eyes, standing on the platform saying your goodbyes and having your conversation suddenly drowned out when the engine let off steam . . . but we loved our steam engines for themselves, and were sad to see them go when the diesels took over in the 1960s. The LCGB plate - meaning Locomotive Club of Great Britain - tells us that this is not a regular service train, but a Special, so the crowd on the platform is likely to be composed mainly of trainspotters. Gloucester used to be served by the Great Western Railway and the Midland Railway, each with their own station; the old Midland station later provided the site for an Asda superstore. Both companies had excellent reputations, but some steam enthusiasts will assert that the Great Western, developed by the pioneering Victorian engineer Brunel, was responsible for producing some of the greatest steam engines ever built. Locomotive No 4079, seen here, is the famous Pendennis Castle, which was built in 1924 and was one of the GWR engines which acquitted itself well in the 1925 locomotive rivalry between the GWR and the LNER. The Pendennis Castle spent the latter years of the 20th century in Australia after being purchased by Rio Tinto Zinc.

S uperimpose this scene on the docks at the beginning of the 21st century, and the good ship Olympia would be nicely moored outside Dr Foster's Liquor Co and Steamboat Willy's, who occupy Kimberley Warehouse at the time of writing. The Port of Gloucester's solidly-constructed warehouses have stood the test of time well; even the lettering of Reynold's Flour Mills which we can see on the photograph on the far warehouse is just as clear as we write, and the Mariners' Church which stands behind it has as many visitors as ever - if not more. There is still plenty of activity around this spot, but in less than half a century the docks have changed completely in character, if not in appearance. The warehouses which were built for grain storage have

taken on a variety of tourist, leisure and administrative uses, and have adapted remarkably well to their new roles as museums and offices. So the docks continue to contribute to the city's economy, although the dockers seen here unloading the motor vessel Olympia's 550 tons of potatoes from Rotterdam, destined for onward despatch to West Midland manufacturers, may well have been horrified at the idea of the docks as a leisure attraction. But there was no reason for them to picture the Port of Gloucester becoming anything other than a thriving port in years to come; trade figures for 1958 had recently been announced, and showed that the volume of cargoes handled at Gloucester that year was double that of the previous year.

Above: 'Re-instate the basic petrol ration and ease public transport', is the message of this post-war Basic Petrol Protest Rally. Petrol had been one of the first commodities to go on ration when war was declared in 1939, with the petrol allocation for private individuals set so low that many cars were soon taken off the road and spent the war propped up on bricks with their wheels off. By the time peace returned, people were looking forward eagerly to the end of petrol rationing along with all other forms of rationing. Unfortunately shortages did not end overnight, and the Government, faced with the urgent task of rebuilding the country's economy, was keen to ensure that such raw materials as were available went primarily to industry. So, as far as the public was concerned, not only were we stuck with our ration books for some while yet, but some things were actually going to become even more scarce before the situation finally began to ease - and petrol was one of them. In September 1947 the Government saw fit to withdraw the basic petrol ration, and the number of protesters who have gathered in (we think) Gloucester Cattle Market tells us just how popular this decision was with Gloucester's motorcyclists! Nor was Gloucester the only town where feelings ran high - the Gloucester and Cotswold Motor Cycle Club's protest rally, organised by Fred Grove, was just one of many similar protests being staged by motor cycle clubs the length and breadth of the country.

Right: Spot the odd one out! Yes, a biker on a BSA C15 has infiltrated the scooters; but that's OK because we are not mods and rockers, we are members of Gloucester's Vespa Club, plus two senior Scouts. And far from looking for aggro, we are about to set off on a ride through the streets of Gloucester to advertise Christian Aid week. Scooters first became popular immediately after the war, especially among young people who found them a convenient and affordable form of independent transport; when the Suez crisis pushed petrol up to a horrifying six shillings a gallon (about 6p a litre), their low fuel consumption made them even more attractive. As we can see from our photograph, a comparatively large proportion of scooter riders were girls; during the late 1950s the secretary of the Gloucester branch of the Vespa Club of Great Britain was a young lady named Doreen Teague, and she was one of four ladies and fourteen gentlemen who donned Union Jacks and represented Great Britain at the 1959 Euro Vespa Rally in Paris. The Italian Vespa - meaning Wasp - first went on sale in Britain in 1946, and within a decade more than a million Piaggio Vespas had been sold nationwide. The best-selling British-made scooter was the 249cc BSA Sunbeam, launched in 1958, but for the vast majority of people, scooter remained synonymous with Vespa.

On the home front

*T****his page and overleaf:*** *The end of the second world war did not mean that the Civil Defence no longer had an important role to play in civilian life. Catastrophes occur in peacetime as well, in the form of floods, fires and explosions, so it was important that each town and city knew how to cope in any such emergency. On a more sinister note still, more mature readers will remember that during the middle decades of the 20th century tensions were running high as a result of the so-called Cold War between Russia and America, and there were very real fears that the button might be pushed at any time and we would be plunged into nuclear war. However, it was always comforting to know that if the worst happened and the world crumbled around our ears, the ladies from the Welfare Section of the Civil Defence knew what do in an emergency and would be on hand to pour us a nice cup of tea! Exercises were held by the Civil Defence, such as exercise 'Eastwold' which involved a rescue party from Stroud and a number of other local members of the Gloucestershire Civil Defence (pictured right).*

From previous page: One group you could rely on to be present at every exercise were the ladies who, whatever the circumstances, could conjure up warm drinks and something to eat. The Ministry of Food, recognising that this group had a potentially invaluable role to play in ensuring the survival of the nation, offered staff development in the form of a comprehensive post-war programme of emergency feeding training exercises. These were held at strategic locations up and down the country - locally, Cranham was one of the venues - and the idea was that delegates from nearby local authorities would attend these courses, and would then pass the training on to Welfare teams in their own community. The exercises took place in the open air, often on a piece of waste ground, perhaps an old bombsite, and typically the delegates would be presented with a heap of the kind of rubble which would be readily available almost anywhere - odd bricks, empty tins, bits of metal and a dustbin lid or two - and shown how to turn them into an emergency cooker, which basically meant improvising some kind of contraption with a place to light a

fire, a chimney to let the smoke out, and somewhere to put the cooking utensils. The relief on the faces of this row of worthy local ladies standing triumphantly behind their pans shows that they have managed it - in fact they are smiling so broadly that one suspects they have had quite a lot of fun in the process!

taff at Gloucester's telephone exchange have got their Christmas trimmings up, and are doing their best not to be put off by the fact that a civic delegation is looking over their shoulders. The Post Office telephone operators had found themselves much in the limelight in 1959; not only did Gloucester open the extension to its exchange in Bull Street to provide a better service for its 5,500-plus subscribers, but the Postmaster General, Mr Ernest Marples, decided that it was time for the telephone service to cultivate a new 'be-more-friendly' image. Until then, operators had all been taught to adhere rigidly to the responses prescribed in the Post Office phrase manual, which told them the exact words to say in every conceivable situation, from instructing callers to have their coins ready,

right through to pushing button B. To depart from the formula was unthinkable; if the book told you to say, 'Please put the coins in the box', then you would not dream of saying, 'Put the coins in the box please'. Suddenly, shock horror! it was OK to change the script slightly; it was even OK to say good morning to callers - although it was not OK to have long discussions about the weather or Emergency Ward Ten. Wouldn't it be nice if BT's 21st-century electronic voices occasionally surprised us with a friendly comment? Another aspect of the new 1959 image was that the politically correct term for the telephoning public was changed from 'subscribers' to 'customers' - although thankfully it was not yet time for the operators themselves to become 'human resources'.

Around the city centre

There is a lot to be said for shopping centres: they are dry and warm even in the bitterest weather, and there is no traffic to contend with. But Christmas shopping in the old streets used to have its own kind of magic. When it got dark, the Christmas illuminations and the extravagant displays in the shop windows were a marvellous sight, turning the whole of the city centre into a blaze of light against the night sky. The atmosphere was terrific; you togged up in woolly gloves, hats and scarves, and you could see your breath in the air like smoke, but jostling your way through the crowds laden with parcels and eating hot chestnuts as you queued for the bus kept you warm. In 1965 Gloucester spent £3,000 on illuminations to make its streets look festive, with Christmas trees, stars and strings of coloured lights strung high above the streets. Then on New Year's Eve, as midnight approached, traffic would be diverted away from The Cross so that revellers could gather here to see the New Year in. At midnight bells pealed, train whistles blew, and hooters, buzzers and sirens sounded all over the City; and The Cross would erupt with exuberant cheering and singing as the huge crowds who had travelled in from all parts of Gloucester saw in another year.

Below: Wasn't it easier to tell one car from another, in the days when you could drive down Northgate Street? There is no mistaking the Hillman Imp seen here. They were quirky little cars. The motoring press loved them; engines with overhead camshafts were still relatively new and were considered far superior to the old push-rod engines, and the Imp was the lowest-priced vehicle with an overhead-cam engine. In 1965, the year of our picture, a new one cost £501-1s-3d (£420 plus purchase tax). Imps were nippy, but to the non-technically minded they took a bit of getting used to. To begin with they kept their engines - which were aluminium and therefore lighter - in the back. How many petrol pump attendants walked round and round the car, looking for somewhere to stick the nozzle? In fact petrol went in at the front, under the 'bonnet' which was in this case the boot. Owners using them to transport personal possessions might also have found it was not advisable to put one's cherished vinyl collection at the rear of the passenger compartment, as the heat from the engine caused the records to warp gently over a long journey. And in the days when car servicing was more of an ad hoc, do-it-yourself business than it is now, many an unwary owner must have discovered that aluminium engines have prima donna tendencies, so that if, for instance, you forgot to put your antifreeze in, you were likely to find yourself with a warped cylinder head after the first frosty night.

By the mid-1960s people all over the country were buying cars. Signs of the times in this picture include the prominent advertisement for Vauxhall-Bedford dealers Hough and Whitmore, the bridge across London Road which serves as an advertisement for Lockheed brakes, and the learner driver who is no doubt wishing the policemen on bicycles were not so close. The number of cars in Britain was rapidly approaching the 10 million mark, and in Gloucester as elsewhere more and more young people were learning to drive; passing your test had become practically a rite of passage for the younger generation by the end of the decade. Readers who learned to drive in that era were taught hand-signals - and didn't you feel stupid, sticking your arm straight out to turn right, rotating it in huge circles to turn left, and flapping up and down when you had to slow down or stop! It wasn't dignified, and you were keenly aware that few people who had passed their test bothered with hand-signals. In fact a significant proportion of the older drivers on the roads at that time had managed to escape without ever taking a test. The driving test was first introduced in 1935 on a voluntary basis, and it then became compulsory for everybody who had taken out their first driving licence since 1st April 1934. Initially the Driving Test Organisation set the test fee at 7s 6d (37.5 pence), thinking this would comfortably cover its administration costs; however, so many people sent in their seven-and-sixpences that it made a profit of £16,000 - and reduced the fee.

Money has been the cause of many a family row. How much you spend, what you spend it on, why you haven't got any left, and how much you owe - they are all sensitive subjects. In post-war Britain, the question of whether or not you should buy on credit became something of a source of friction between the generations. Many older people had been brought up not to get anything 'on tick' if they could possibly help it; 'neither a lender nor a borrower be' was an oft-quoted maxim. Then suddenly banks, finance companies and retailers were all encouraging us to buy now and pay later. If we liked the look of a carpet in the City Carpet Co's window in Westgate Street, there was a tempting notice inviting us to pay on 'easy terms'. In fact, provided we had a bank account and a job we could probably have furnished the whole house on HP, and bought a car too if we wanted; but the idea horrified those brought up in a culture where debt was considered almost immoral. For the unwary, of course, it was easy to get deep into debt, and a decade or so later when plastic currency first became widespread another generation of young adults was to face a similar pitfall with credit cards. Domestic finances were becoming more sophisticated, and were to grow more sophisticated still; telephone and internet banking are a far cry from the days when people used to set great store upon knowing their bank manager personally.

Above: Some elements here have changed, but some haven't. Younger readers will be forgiven for thinking that the Golden Anchor was a pub - it certainly looks like one! but in fact it was an outfitters. Next door, in the fine building which was once Robert Raikes' home and which has become a pub in more recent times, British Relay is proudly announcing BBC2 - Here Now! From its inception, BBC2, the nation's third channel, was intended to cater for minority interests. In the mid-1960s, a three-channel GEC television set cost 61 guineas cash - this was of course still black and white. Many people simply did not believe that one day viewers would be able to receive pictures in colour, in their own living-rooms; the notion seemed too far-fetched. Even if it happened one day, it would surely not be in their lifetime - after all, having television at all still seemed like a miracle! It was hard to adjust to the breakneck speed at which science and technology was racing forward, and certainly older people had a great deal to cope with around that time - new technology, new currency and a society with changing values. . . Beyond Robert Raikes' house, the New County Hotel - once called the Ram Hotel - has changed little between the photograph and the writing, but the once-familiar name of Foyles has disappeared.

Right: The Co-operative movement made a very real difference to the lives of the workers throughout the first part of the 20th century, bringing them everyday goods at prices they could afford. During the closing decades of the 19th century local co-operative societies were being formed in towns and cities all over the country, and Gloucester was no exception: the Gloucester Co-operative and Industrial Society was started by a group of local working men, and opened its first shop in Prince Street in August 1860. Its membership grew rapidly and it operated more and more shops around the area, including the one at Co-op Corner and the other large stores in Brunswick Road. The Co-op store pictured here is Branch Number 10 at 106-108 High Street, Tredworth, opened in 1888. Rochdale is widely regarded as the place where the Co-operative movement all began, and certainly it was the Rochdale Pioneers who in the mid-19th century introduced the system of dividend payments which became one of the Co-op's great attractions. Each family's divi number was permanently etched into the memories of even its youngest member, to be quoted whenever they made any purchase, however small - it all adds up! In addition to its retail outlets, the Co-op also helped working families immeasurably through its insurance and funeral services; by paying in a modest amount each week, people were assured of a decent burial and some degree of financial support in case of need, and this gave them peace of mind.

Below: This photograph of Westgate Street was taken in 1959 and shows a varied collection of delivery vehicles of the day. Of particular interest to transport enthusiasts is the little three-wheeled truck outside the Theatre Vaults public house next to Woolworths, which we believe to be a Scammel Mechanical Horse. As the name implies, the three-wheeler cabs were intended to be a direct replacement for a horse, and it was actually possible to attach a dray. These odd, unconventional little vehicles stayed around for a surprisingly long time. They were not powerful enough to pull heavy loads - any more than the horse which they replaced could - but their single front wheel gave them a very small turning circle so that - again, like a horse - they could be turned round in narrow streets where conventional larger lorries would find it difficult to manoeuvre. Turning our attention back to the shops, just beyond the Theatre Vaults at the time of the photograph was one of Gloucester's long-established family businesses, seed merchants G Winfield & Son, who had been trading from this spot since the 19th century. Restoration work was carried out at their premises in 1959, which probably explains the presence of

the scaffolding; a half-timbered structure with ancient woodwork and some 300-year-old windows were revealed, and at the time of writing part of the old structure, with G Winfield's name inscribed upon it, can easily be seen if you cast your eyes down the passageway adjoining number 26.

Bottom: Take away the cars, change the names on the businesses and this view has changed little over the decades since our photograph was taken. Westgate Street used to be the busiest shopping street in Gloucester; however, alterations to the road layout and the development of shopping centres at the other side of the city have taken away the hustle and bustle and turned this end of the street into something of a backwater. The County Council annex was constructed in the early 1960s. Years before, Woods Army & Navy Stores had occupied this spot, but towards the end of the 1940s Woods moved across to the opposite side of Westgate Street. The church of St Nicholas has been redundant for many years at the time of writing. It dates back to the 12th century and its spire was originally over 200 feet in height but the top part sustained a direct hit

from Royallist artillery during the Seige of Gloucester in 1643. Although the damage was repaired the spire became unstable and was reduced to about half its original height in 1783 and the ball cap was added. A number of the city's church towers and spires have been afflicted by subsidence at one time or another, and St Nicholas' was no exception; it is reported that early in the 20th century Sir Francis Fox, who was famous for carrying out remedial work to save Winchester Cathedral, was called upon to prevent St Nicholas' tower and spire from collapsing - which he did by pumping vast quantities of concrete into the walls and foundations.

Christmas decorations across Barton Street (now Eastgate Street) tell us that the festive season is approaching again. How many lucky children over the years found a bicycle from T G Hall's under the Christmas tree? In Hall's window are advertisements for Sturmey Archer and Raleigh, familiar names to many generations of cyclists; though in the very early days of cycling, dealers used to build their own bicycles from components supplied by various manufacturers, rather than simply buying and selling pre-assembled machines. Bicycles of the early 1900s had a number of refinements which would strike modern cyclists as quaint; ladies' bikes, for instance, had netting fitted to the rear mudguard to cover the top part of the back wheel, so that the ladies' skirts did not catch in the spokes. On the other hand, our predecessors would have been puzzled by our heavy-duty locking devices; they used to leave their bikes propped up against a wall all day, and return to find them still there, complete with wheels and saddlebag. Many readers will not remember the shop next door to T G Hall being anything other than a jewellers. It has belonged to Donald Judd for a long time; at the time of writing it is occupied by Brownings, who took over from James F Payne. Before James Payne came Maurice Wilkes, and before that, briefly, Callaghan & Cale. Earlier still, as we see here, it used to be Carltons boot repairers.

Above: To the right of our picture stands the imposing facade of the Theatre de Luxe - but a facade was exactly what it was by the time this photograph was taken in the late 1950s. In fact the theatre had been destroyed by fire one cold January morning in 1939. The blaze took hold during the early hours, and in spite of the valiant efforts of Gloucester Fire Brigade it continued to rage for some two hours, consuming the cinema organ, the seating, the stage and most of the building's interior. Nearby residents were awoken and evacuated, but in fact the firefighters managed to prevent the flames spreading to the surrounding buildings. By the time the fire was extinguished, all that remained was the shell. The front part of the building was still pretty much intact, and was retained as the street front when rebuilding was carried out. The classical portico which we see had been added to the cinema in 1922. The cinema itself was opened in 1909; before that the building had been used as an assembly room, and earlier still it had been a piano factory belonging to Frederick Goddard. However, the notice on the side of the TGWU building - once the Gloucester Coffee House - warns that developers have their eye on this corner. Shortly afterwards this corner was completely transformed, and what was left of the old Theatre de Luxe finally bit the dust.

Right: A number of improvements, both aesthetic and practical, have been carried out at The Cross since this photograph was taken. On the practical side, excluding through traffic from this area solved the potentially serious problems which pedestrians used to face at Mann's Corner. As we can see on this photograph, the pavement at this spot simply was not wide enough for people walking two abreast to pass each other; and as it became blocked, pedestrians used to step out into the roadway to bypass the congestion. The Council scratched its head over this problem for many years; it thought of taking the building line in Eastgate Street back to make the pavement wider, and it thought of creating a pedestrian walkway through St Michael's tower. In the event, pedestrianisation brought by far the best solution. The new layout of the town, with the shopping centres bringing the bulk of shoppers to the Eastgate Street area, has rather taken away the impact of The Cross, which used to be the focal point of the City where the two main roads crossed. However, St Michael's Tower, having served briefly as the Tourist Information Office, has become quite a tourist attraction in its own right, and, together with the other interesting historic and artistic features which are to be found nearby, serves to remind us of the traditional importance of this spot.

Westgate is changing. Saunders' erstwhile neighbour has gone, and suddenly you can walk out of the Shire Hall and look straight across at the Cathedral. Until the late 1950s a building once occupied by the Shire Hall Restaurant stood adjacent to Saunders; more recently the gap has been filled by a brick building, so that neither the Cathedral nor the side of this attractive building is still visible from our photographer's viewpoint. Relatively few of Gloucester's old timber-framed houses still survive. No doubt there were sound practical reasons for replacing them, but when we look at those which have made it into the 21st century, we cannot help but appreciate their timeless elegance which never loses its appeal. The city centre is an eclectic mix of buildings. Alongside its abundance of fine ecclesiastical architecture, it can offer us everything from stately banks of the late 19th century and imposing edifices put up by retailers such as the Co-operative and Bon Marche in the early 20th century, to successful, hi-tec modern complexes created in more recent years. Interspersed with all this are some impressive public buildings, a number of old cottages and, unfortunately, a few examples of the box-like structures which were in vogue during the 1960s but which very soon began to look dated.

At leisure

Below: They sometimes say you can judge how civilised a society is by how it treats its more vulnerable members; and on that basis, Gloucester scores pretty highly here. In 1959 Gloucester's Old People's Clubs organised a holiday for their members, and the happy smiling faces captured on this snapshot are just a section of the 120 elderly people who were off for a week in Paignton in May. They stayed in hotels just a few yards from the beach which would normally have charged between 10 and 12 guineas for the week, but thanks to some keen negotiating by the organisers each member had to pay just £6 - which included not only the week's accommodation but also coach travel, boat trips, admission to the pier, and deck chairs on the beach. They were accompanied by a band of volunteers who went at their own expense, and we can safely say that a good time was had by all: they paddled, they sat on the beach in the sunshine, they enjoyed concerts put on for them by Paignton's Social Services, they walked along the cliff and looked through the penny-in-the-slot telescopes . . . In short, they did all the things you would expect senior citizens to do, plus some that you wouldn't - the chaps played football, and both sexes played cricket! The holiday was a great success, and we would like to bet that more than one reader will have photographs in their own family album taken at Paignton in May 1959.

Right: Schoolchildren love school trips, and these pupils from St Paul's Junior School, Gloucester, seem to have been favoured with a sunny day for theirs. Of all the destinations for children's outings within day-trip distance of Gloucester, Dudley Zoo has to have been one of the most popular with successive generations of youngsters, and that is where our photograph was taken. No doubt a number of readers will have assembled in this very spot with their classmates and teacher, and said 'cheese' for the photographer just as we see this class doing. Before David Attenborough's wildlife documentaries brought wild animals complete with their natural habitats into our living rooms, zoos were the only opportunity most people had to actually see wild animals and to appreciate their grace, their beauty and the sheer power and character that can never be fully conveyed by photographs in a book. Opened in 1937, Dudley Zoo prided itself on the many different species of animal which it contained: in 1950 it had no less than 800 creatures of 175 different species, not counting the occupants of the aquarium. Thousands of children from all over the country were fascinated by Snappy the Californian sealion and Meena and Ranee the elephants. Some of the little faces on this photograph look a shade apprehensive; perhaps they have been told a cautionary tale about what happens to little girls and boys who tease the lions - or perhaps they are just screwing up their eyes against the bright May sunshine!

Bottom: Valentines young and not-so-young are dancing the night away at the tenth 'Old Ben' St Valentine's Ball at the Guildhall in February 1959. As we can see from the crowded dance-floor, Gloucester's romantics showed up in force, and some couples had to be turned away when all 300 tickets had gone. The ball was arranged by the Newsvendors' Benevolent and Provident Association - hence the name Old Ben - and the money raised went to retired newsvendors. It was a smart occasion, strictly suit and tie for men and evening dress for ladies; many of the ladies have wisely brought an evening shawl to keep their shoulders warm. Dress code was more formal then. Designer casualwear had not been invented to confuse the distinction between what was smart and what was not, and there would certainly have been no need for a bouncer on the door to sieve out anyone trying to get in without a jacket and tie, or wearing jeans and trainers. However, the teenage revolution, with its new American-influenced fashions in clothes, speech, manners and music, was not very far away. Already by the late 50s it was becoming the norm for bands to include rock and roll sequences in amongst the jazz and the traditional waltzes and foxtrots, and some of us were jiving and rock-and-rolling - while others of us were so shocked by Elvis Presley's obscene gyrating hips that we wanted nothing to do with rock and roll and sat those dances out, returning to the floor when the band struck up something a little more to our taste.

Right: We have included this picture for its charm. Although taken in Coleford, it emphasises the area's agricultural heritage, traditionally attached great importance to Harvest Festival celebrations. From mid-September, many processions such as the one seen here were to be seen in Gloucester itself and in the surrounding villages, wending their way to local churches for special Harvest Home services. This particular photograph was taken in Coleford, and shows an extremely impressive procession which by all accounts was more than 300 yards long. With families of all denominations represented, the procession is on its way to Coleford Baptist Church; the girls in their Sunday frocks and white ankle socks make a charming sight, and those vegetables are fine specimens too. Not only did Gloucester take a quite justified pride in its vegetables and flowers, but flower arranging was always a serious matter too - a point which was proved conclusively by the Gloucester and District Flower Arrangement Society in the mid 20th century. When the society was founded in 1956, a certain gentleman rather unwisely made a disparaging comment in public to the effect that in his opinion it would not last three months. This gentleman had to eat his opinion two years later when the Society put on a two-day exhibition at the New Inn; the exhibition was opened by Lady Boyce, a total of 250 tickets were sold, and there were 180 exhibits on display by 54 members.

This charming scene was captured on the rectory lawn at Littledean. The dancers are all members of the Gloucester Association of Church Youth Groups, and part of the reason for so many colourful, swirling skirts is that this gathering is part of a week-long programme of events with a gipsy theme, culminating in a grand fete at St Aldate's Church on the Saturday. It has to be said that the young people on this photograph - taken on the Tuesday - are not in much danger of being mistaken for gipsies; however, the overall effect is very pleasing. A barbecue has been put on for them, and in between the rock and roll sessions they can go and sit round the campfire and refresh themselves with hot-dogs and a drink. American influence was strong during the late 50s, particularly amongst teenagers, and we guess that the dance numbers on this occasion included a high proportion of hits from across the Atlantic. No doubt they danced to Bill Haley and the Comets' 1955 classic 'Rock Around The Clock', along with songs from other American rock and roll stars like the Platters, Buddy Holly whose career came to an untimely end in 1959, and the youthful Elvis; while Richie Valens' 'Donna' and Connie Francis' 'Who's Sorry Now?' were good songs for a smooch. Altogether some 200 young people came along to this event, and evidently had a terrific time. Good music, pleasant company, lovely weather and beautiful surroundings - what more could anyone ask for?

What better way to end a party than with a sing-song around the piano! Singing their hearts out here are the children who have just enjoyed a festive feast at the Midway Lodge (8260) RAOB Christmas party at Cainscross. A number of the boys appear to be singing so clearly that we suspect they may well be choirboys, while a couple of the little ones are too shy to open their mouths - tongue-tied by the presence of the cameraman, perhaps. No doubt Mr Bert Jeffries, on the piano (at the keyboard, that is - the name of the young gentleman sitting on top of the piano is not recorded) is giving them a good selection of favourite carols, with maybe a popular song or two mixed in. The Christmas number one that year was not a seasonal song - it was in fact Conway Twitty's It's Only Make Believe - but the previous year a real Christmas classic had topped the charts in November and stayed there all over Christmas and the New Year: Harry Belafonte, singing Mary's Boy Child. It is a song that has been handed down the generations, and we would be surprised if these youngsters had not sung it at some stage in the proceedings. 'Hark, now hear the angels sing, a new King born today . . .'

Above: Railways used to exercise the same fascination over the average small boy as do virtual reality spaceships and extra-terrestrial aliens these days. What better way to spend a wet Sunday afternoon than working out a new layout for your Hornby set? The living-room floor became a complex system of curves, points, signals, stations, platforms and sidings. You were unlikely to let your little sister into the room, but you always asked Dad to help because you knew how disappointed he would be if you didn't - grown men enjoy playing with trains as much as little boys do. On this photograph, which was taken at a Gloucester Carnival, the men are managing to restrain themselves and let the little ones go first, and this very fine model railway run by Mr R F G Porter is proving popular with the girls as well as the boys. Another Gloucester man who never lost his passion for model railways was Post Office engineer Mr Jim West; Jim devoted years during the late 1940s and early 50s to building a model locomotive to scale from drawings obtained from the railway company. Through their hobby men such as these

two brought pleasure to countless children all over the Gloucester area. One imagines that children born into the third millennium and surrounded from birth by push-button hi-tec entertainment may at some stage begin to wonder what on earth their predecessor used to do, in the dim and distant days before computers and even television were invented: well, they used to have fun, is the answer!

Top: Although we cannot be sure of the exact circumstances which saw these mirthful schoolboys leaping into the swimming pool with such enthusiasm, we guess they may well be taking part in the annual water sports competitions which were an important feature of the school year for many generations of Gloucester schoolchildren. Gloucester Baths echoed to excited shouts of encouragement and cheers for the winners on numerous occasions every July as local schools, including the Crypt Grammar School and King's School, staged their swimming galas there. A few schools were lucky enough to have their own pools, and other schools on the outskirts of the city would stage similar events at their local baths. With Britain's Anita Lonsborough poised to win the gold in the 200 metres breaststroke at the 1960 Olympics, swimming became a very popular sport indeed around this time. The city invested in new public baths in the mid-1960s, constructing a swimming pool in Barton Street, next to the old; at the time of writing this site is once more being redeveloped. The main pool of the old baths, built in 1891, continued to be used as a training pool. How many readers can still remember spending their first ever swimming lesson there cowering down the shallow end, cold, shivering and terrified of letting go of the rail; then gaining confidence and managing a breadth, then a length, then perhaps going on to get their Third, Second or even First Class certificate?

Bird's eye view

All was not well at Gloster Aircraft Company in the late 1950s, but that did not prevent them from showing their fighting spirit - in the shape of their last fighting Gladiator. GAC's Apprentice School had been busy restoring this great machine to pre-war condition, complete with radio, instruments, gunsight, and four 303 Browning machine guns. 'Gloster's Flying Museum Piece', as some people termed it, was 20 years old, and once the apprentices had finished overhauling and re-equipping it, it became the country's only Gladiator fighter plane in serviceable condition. The Gladiator was one of the exhibits which enthralled thousands of spectators at the Staverton air display, along the most modern jet aircraft and the daredevil antics of the formation aerobatics teams. GAC's troubles, which were universally shared by the people of Gloucester, stemmed from the Government's new defence programme; once their contract to supply Javelins came to an end, there would, it was feared, be no more government work for GAC. Inevitably there were redundancies, and the future of the company hung in the balance for a long time as a succession of official statements came out, variously telling GAC that it must find work for itself either inside or outside the aircraft construction industry, then promising assistance, then reassessing the situation, then quoting more facts and figures . . and all the while men's livelihoods were at stake.

> *The railway track can be seen following the road past the park to Barton Street and the infamous Barton Gates*

*L*ooking down on Gloucester from the air, we can see that tents and marquees are up in the Park, suggesting that fun and frolics of some kind - perhaps as part of the Carnival - are afoot. This view dates from the mid-60s, when the railway line still ran to Tuffley, and the track can be seen cutting across the photograph following the line of the road past the park and along to Barton Street, which it crossed by means of a level crossing - the infamous Barton Gates. The section of road between here and the corner of Brunswick Road used to be a continuation of Barton Street, but since the construction of the shopping centre it has become part of Eastgate Street and been re-numbered accordingly, so that, for instance, the old number 29 Barton Street has become 87 Eastgate Street. Many familiar landmarks can be picked out, with the Cathedral and the Docks being particularly prominent from the air.

Memories of GLOUCESTER

The line of the canal, with the Severn meandering off to the right and the docks easily identifiable, instantly gives us our bearings for this aerial view of Gloucester. The prominent chimney to the right is that of Castle Meads Power Station, which no longer exists. Running up the photograph from The Cross, near

the bottom and just right of centre, is Southgate Street, which then sweeps round to become the A430 Bristol Road beyond the bowling and putting greens at the Spa. A short distance up from this spot, on the left hand side of the road, Moreland's factory was still in full production when this photograph was taken. A comparison with a modern

aerial map will immediately show us that closer to the city centre a few important link roads are still missing. Southgate Street was at this time still the main north-south route through the city, carrying traffic right down to The Cross; today, most of those tiny dots which we can see making their way down the lower part of the photograph would have headed off round the inner ring road. Further to the left, Brunswick Road runs parallel with Southgate Street, and the Library building can be picked out, with the Technical College behind it. Along Eastgate Street, approximately midway between Brunswick Road and Southgate Street, the roof of the Market is clearly visible.

Sporting life

Schoolboys come in two varieties: the ones who like sports, and the ones who don't. For the latter category, school cross-countries were a thing to be dreaded, and if you could develop a severe cold the day before, or, even better, twist your ankle, then you thanked your lucky stars that you were off the hook - this time. However, there have always been plenty of boys of the sporting variety in Gloucester, and during the spring and summer months a spirit of keen competition developed at the various schools. Juniors and seniors at King's and the other local schools would train hard for their school's annual cross-country race (five miles for the seniors, less for the juniors) through fields, woods, and usually a fair bit of mud; then there were the Cross Country Area Championships to aim for, with Gloucester's schoolboys competing for a place in the North Gloucestershire team which would go on to meet the team from South Gloucestershire. And there was no need to abandon competitive athletics when you left school; adult competitors too regularly pounded through the city centre, with walking as well as running races a regular feature on the city's calendar. The annual Whitsun Road Race always attracted a good entry, and crowds of all ages turned out to cheer on their friends and relatives. Although we cannot confirm the exact occasion pictured here, nor identify Number 22, we join the spectators in applauding his stamina.

having steadfastly resisted takeover bids by larger companies. Pat Onions had bought the company from Bill Cotton in 1964, and he went on to concentrate on making competition trial bikes. During the mid-1970s the firm had three models on the market and exported around 80 per cent of their output; the Enduro, a dual-purpose trials/road machine, was especially popular in the USA.

Top: Before hunting became something of a national hot potato, Boxing Day meets used to draw huge crowds - and no hint of trouble. Local hunts included the Ledbury Hounds, the Berkeley Hounds, and the Cotswold Vale Farmers' Hunt which is featured here. It was very unusual indeed for the meet to be held in the middle of Gloucester, but on this occasion it was; our photograph was taken just outside the New Inn, a very appropriate setting. The Master, Mr J P Sherwin, took the pack into the inn courtyard, where the traditional stirrup cup was drunk. Thousands of people thronged Northgate Street to catch a glimpse of the colourful spectacle - the red-coated huntsmen, the alert, eager hounds and the glossy, immaculately-groomed horses resplendent in their highly-polished hunting tack. At eleven o'clock the hunting horn sounded, hounds emerged into Northgate Street, supervised by whipper-in Mr Bill Darke, and not for many decades had Northgate Street echoed to the thunder of so many horses' hooves, as the hundred or so riders set off for Sandhurst - leaving the spectators to disperse and, we guess, go home to a Boxing Day lunch of cold turkey. Some years later, in January 1964, the Cotswold Vale hunt again made history by holding the first ever meet in Gloucester's cattle market.

Above: Spectating at a motorcycle scrambling event is a great way of spending an afternoon for all the family - just as long as sun is shining and the ground is dry, so that you're not in constant danger of being spattered with mud. For this particular event in May 1961 the weather looks just about perfect. The Gloucester and Cotswold motor cycle club began scrambling in 1929; the regular Bank Holiday events held at its track at Tirley attracted riders from all parts of the country and produced such local heroes as Billy Jackson, Jim Timms, and Mike Smith - seen here riding a Cotton motorcycle. Cotton was a small Gloucester motorcycle manufacturing firm started by Bill Cotton, possibly as early as 1919; more than 50 years later, when other famous British motorcycle manufacturers such as Francis Barnett and James had ceased to exist, Cotton was still turning out a handful of bikes a week,

Above: The final of the 1959 Rugby County Championship was played at Bristol between Gloucestershire and Warwickshire. Fans who had travelled from Gloucester must have been biting their nails towards the end of the match when their team was trailing 9-11, with the final whistle in sight. Unfortunately their hopes were then dashed as Warwickshire's Ricky Melville scored his second try of the match, bringing the final score to 14-9. Younger readers may question the mathematics of this, but older readers will recall that an unconverted try used to be worth only three points; the scoring system was changed to encourage players to concentrate on getting more tries instead of relying on penalty goals to bring them points. The pattern of play has evolved in a number of ways over the years; for instance, there used to be many more set-pieces, and it was not so easy for a team to win a line-out on their own throw, because lifting fellow team members who were jumping for the ball was not allowed. A study of the line-out in this photograph leaves us musing that either the numbering on the shirts was not on the usual system, or the scrum-half and stand-off half (numbers 9 and 10) were in a very strange position! In conclusion, however, we have great satisfaction in reporting that Gloucestershire got their revenge upon Warwickshire in 1972, beating them 11-6 at Coventry to win the Championship.

Above right: What a different atmosphere from the present day! Twenty-first century supporters would be less formally dressed, and a lot more animated. The rows of people standing in their overcoats look more as if they were attending a funeral. Of course, if they were supporting Gloucester

in this particular game, perhaps that is rather how they felt. This match between Gloucester and Hereford United at Longlevens on 7th March 1959 was probably one which Gloucester's young goalkeeper would prefer to forget; Wilkinson, who had recently joined the team from Bristol City, let in a total of six goals - though he did manage some saves too. The result was Gloucester City 0 - Hereford United 6. Gloucester played at Longlevens from 1935 until the early 1960s, when the site was sold for housing and the club went to Horton Road in 1964; from there they moved to Meadow Park, which has seating for 560 and covered standing for 2,000, with a total capacity of 5,000. Gloucester, it has to be said, takes its rugby more seriously than its football. Hereford won the League that season and went on to be elected to the Football League in 1972 after beating First Division Newcastle United whilst still a non-League club. Gloucester City have remained in the Southern League ever since.
Gloucester City earned their nickname of 'Tigers' in 1980 when their colours changed from red and white to yellow and black.

Supporters of Gloucester RFC in the 1950s and 60s are likely to recognise a familiar face or two on this photograph: getting stuck in are the former Gloucester skipper Cyril Thomas, Bill Patteson, and George Hastings who was capped 13 times for England. The Pontypool scrum-half who has just got the ball away from a line-out before being tackled is C Evans, who was capped once for Wales in their match against England in 1960. Those who do remember the 1950s/60s era may also regret some of the develop- ments which have come about in the sport as a result of professionalism and leagues. Money has changed various aspects of the game, from admission prices to player loyalties. And if young rugby fans imagine that just because all Rugby Union matches used to be called 'friendlies', the competition was not so intense - well, we had better set them right straight away: clubs like Gloucester were every bit as keen to win then as they are now, and 'friendly' was not perhaps the best word to describe the manner in which the game was sometimes played!

Both pictures: The Stroud Week used to be a great occasion for Gloucestershire cricket fans, and supporters from Gloucester who were able to arrange an expedition to Stroud would make something of a holiday of it. Large crowds would regularly turn up at the Erinold ground to enjoy a feast of county cricket; on a Saturday, with the sun shining as it is in this picture taken in 1959, around 5,000 spectators could be expected. The match which is being watched with such rapt attention is, we believe, Gloucester versus Worcestershire, the first of the week's two fixtures; this was immediately followed by Gloucestershire versus Warwickshire, and unfortunately Gloucestershire lost both matches. Worcestershire won the first match by seven wickets after Gloucestershire's second-innings total of 276 left Worcestershire needing just 65 runs to win. In the second match Gloucestershire dominated most of the match, but, largely due a brilliant innings of 182 not out by Warwickshire's Mike Smith, who was of course to go on to captain England later in his career, the home side eventually lost by four wickets. Notwithstanding these disappointing results, cricket

lovers who had travelled to Stroud saw some fine cricket and would certainly have not regretted making the trip. The Gloucestershire team for the second match included some famous names, with no less than six current or future England players: David Allen, Sam Cook, Tom Graveney, Arthur Milton, John Mortimore and David Smith. Tom Graveney left Gloucestershire to play for Worcestershire not long afterwards. With so many outstanding players in the side at that time, Gloucestershire was in fact enjoying a better season than the outcome of their two matches during Stroud Week might suggest; they came second in the County Championship that year, a result which they never improved upon during the 20th century. The golden period of Gloucestershire cricket was rather further back than most of us can remember - though we might recall sitting on our father's or grandfather's knee and listening to cricketing tales from the 1870s and 1880s, when W G Grace was at his prime. W G Grace's famous association with Gloucestershire came to a sour end in 1899, when he resigned his captaincy with the words: ' I have the greatest affection for the county of my birth, but for the Committee as a body, the greatest contempt.'

At work

> *During the late 1960s, many town centre cattle markets had to close*

Although sheep, pigs and cattle accounted for the majority of the livestock sold at Gloucester Market, there was also a long tradition of horse trading. Barton Fair, the big annual sheep sale which still takes place in September, had a particularly strong reputation as a place to buy and sell good horses. There were some fears that this tradition would be lost when the market moved to St Oswald's Road, but as our picture shows, it was not; this photograph was taken at the first Barton Sheep Sale to be held in the new market, and the equine side of the business is well represented. As for the sheep, there were over 12,000 of them, accommodated in open and covered pennage. The new market was very spacious, and anticipated the nationwide trend for livestock sales to become concentrated in fewer, larger centres as it became more feasible to transport livestock over long distances by road, using the new motorway networks. Dealers increasingly found it worth their while to travel further to the big sales, with the inevitable result that the small local livestock markets which had been a feature of community life for generations were now sparsely attended, and became run down. During the late 1960s, many town centre cattle markets which were no longer viable had to close.

Children of the mid-20th century may not have had the benefits of modern technology, but they achieved results just the same; here we see the children of Viney Hill School (17 miles west of Gloucester) producing their own magazine, a completely new venture for the school. The magazine's twenty-four pages were filled with stories and sketches produced by the eight to eleven-year-olds, and all the work involved in its production was done, as far as possible, by the children themselves. And it was not just a matter of churning the pages out on a printer, or even photocopying; as we can see, those were the days of stencils and duplicators. Readers who have retired from the teaching profession will probably have vivid memories of trying to produce sets of exam papers on Roneo machines; however, these youngsters seem to be managing perfectly well and not making too much mess either. Other children are busy trimming, sorting and binding, and the tally is being recorded with great efficiency on the production chart - great teamwork! It would be nice to think that some of those magazines have survived, tucked away somewhere with childhood souvenirs - the more so, since Viney Hill School's days were already numbered when this photograph was taken. The school closed at Christmas 1965, and its pupils were split up and dispersed among other local schools.

He may not be a tall chap, but he's got a big voice - and it will travel all the way to Germany! The manager and assistant manager of the Hippodrome, armed with a reel-to-reel tape recorder, are busy putting together a recording of the sounds of Gloucester: the cathedral bells, people in pubs, Christmas shoppers and, of course, the cheery cries of the 'Citizen' and 'Journal' newsvendors. This will go to Germany with the Mayor, Councillor V T G Bennett, when he flies out to visit the Royal Gloucestershire Regiment, stationed at Osnabruck. Also on tape will be messages from the soldiers' families; however big and brave and heroic the Glosters are, they still have mothers and sweethearts who miss them,

especially at Christmas. So our gallant boys will be able to listen to their mums and dads and little brothers and wives or girlfriends - and Mr Bill Davis shouting 'Citizen!' - and will then record their own messages for the folks back home in Gloucester. Relatives will gather in the Hippodrome before Christmas, and the messages from Germany will be played. It is perhaps difficult for us to realise, surrounded as we are by 21st century information and communications technology, just how thrilling it must have been, in the days before it was a simple matter just to pick up the phone or record your own cassette or CD, for families to actually hear the voices of their sons and loved ones, so far away. Certainly it must have brightened up their Christmas enormously.

*I*t must be summer - they're digging the road up again! Motorists down the decades have cursed the roadworks that hold up holiday traffic while family tempers fray and radiators boil over, but civil engineers continue to assure us that there are good reasons why certain types of road resurfacing and infrastructure repairs can only be carried out during the summer months. However, traffic jams in Eastgate Street are, thankfully, a thing of the past. This part of Gloucester is very different in character, though the banks to our right as we look at this photograph have remained solidly unperturbed by all the changes. The National Provincial Bank, which became NatWest, has been

here since 1888. Hardy & Co, across Eastgate Street, was where many a young couple setting up their dream home in the 50s went to look at G-Plan furniture - it was not cheap, but you could save quite a bit if you waited for Hardy's sale. Clearance bargains in 1958 included a fireside chair reduced from £16-1s-6d to £7-9s-6d (£16.07p down to £7.48p); or if you were doing up your spare room, you could choose between a 3ft bedstead at 59/6 in the sale, originally priced at £9-11s-0d, and a 3ft divan, down from 17 guineas (£17/17/-) to 9 guineas. And how about a dressing table reduced from £16-12s-6d to £8-19s-6d, to go with the bed? What bargains there were to be had!

*T*his shows a typical summer scene in Westgate during the late 1950s. Wallace Alex Pennington's antiques shop has since disappeared, as have the once-familiar signs for the two big furniture shops, Hampshire's and Foyles, but the Georgian frontage of number 66 - which at the time of this photograph was occupied by Saunders outfitters - and the distinctive turreted building on the corner of College Street have remained unaltered. Walking past Saunders, away from the camera, we would come to the shop that used to be Hickie & Hickie, piano dealers, for many a year; it is still a music shop at the time of writing, having been taken over by Duck, Son & Pinker in the late 1970s. If we keep walking - perhaps pausing for a look at Foyles' G-Plan furniture - we reach Olivers boot and shoe shop; this old-established Gloucester business has moved away from this spot but inside the shop a stained-glass window has been preserved, reminding us of their occupancy. Further perambulation would bring us to Woolworths, who came to this site in the early 1920s, occupying the former Palace cinema; before becoming a cinema, this building had been the Theatre Royal. Woolworths were to remain there for around half a century.

We might easily be misled into thinking that some terrible act of vandalism is about to take place, and a marvellous Georgian house is shortly to be sent crashing to the ground. However, this is not the case; Boots spent the early 20th century masquerading behind a mock-Georgian frontage put up by them just before the first world war, and during the late 1950s they simply decided to get rid of it. This branch in Northgate Street was not only a chemist's, but a cafe and library as well, and Boots had their own band of musicians to entertain the diners. Boots Cash Chemist, as the company used to be known, was one of the early retail businesses to establish a chain of branches in High Streets all over the country. Having built up their chains from around the early 1900s on, some of these established household names - Boots, Woolworths, Marks and Spencer, British Home Stores, Burton's and W H Smith among them - remained with us throughout the 20th century, while others stayed around a long time and then disappeared. Once-familiar names in Gloucester that will mean nothing to future generations include the Maypole Dairy which used to be down Barton Street, Boots' great rival Timothy White & Taylors, later just Timothy Whites, which was along Westgate Street, the Home & Colonial Stores which used to be near the New Inn in Northgate Street, and The Fifty Shilling Tailor, which used to stand right next door to Boots in Northgate Street.

Nostalgia finds its way into all areas of life, even food! Without embarking on such subjects of 21st century controversy as genetically modified crops and E-numbers, it is safe to say that our diet grew much more varied in the second half of the 20th century. More people holidayed abroad and developed a taste for the exotic, and, as the pattern of retailing changed, such previously unknown produce as aubergines and kiwi fruit began to appear on the supermarket shelves. Even the potato began to face competition as one of our main 'staples'; curry houses opened and rice became popular, Italian restaurants came onto the scene and we began buying pasta, and more recently other products such as couscous and polenta have found their way onto many a dinner-table. But there will always be a place on the menu for the versatile spud. Chipped, it has been an essential part of the nation's favourite dish since the 1920s, when a portion of fish and chips cost tuppence - but if you had either not much appetite or not much money, you could ask for a ha'porth of each. Surprisingly, it was not until the mid-1930s that we really began growing potatoes in this country; prior to that all potatoes had been imported from Ireland, Jersey or the Continent - in the case of our photograph, Holland. Apparently there used to be keen competition among the potato merchants to be the first to get their first consignment of new potatoes from Brittany - much like the race to be first with the Beaujolais Nouveau!

*T*he paving slabs have been displaced not by workmen, but by water which gushed out of a burst water main. The burst happened - as catastrophes do - during the early hours of the morning, causing flooding to business premises near Barton Gates, with Matthews & Harris furniture shop bearing the brunt. As far as records go back, parts of Gloucester have been under water rather more regularly than inhabitants would have liked; the most infamous floods of the 20th century were those of 1947, when a rapid thaw of several inches of snow on the uplands coincided with another 6ins of rainfall and resulted in a depth gauge reading of an unprecedented 25ft 6ins at Gloucester, 6ft higher than the previous record set in 1852. The City

Council mounted an emergency operation to provide accommodation for those who had to abandon their homes and to distribute candles, matches, food and coal, the latter being required both for cooking where the gas had failed and for drying out houses. When the floodwaters subsided they also gave out bleach powder and instructed householders to wash down the floors and put bleach down the toilet, to prevent disease. At least on the occasion pictured here the floodwaters were straight out of the mains, rather than dirty Severn water - though this is unlikely to have been of much consolation to the owners of the businesses affected, nor for the morning rush-hour traffic, which was delayed around Barton Gates for even longer than usual.

Left: The Port of Gloucester played a significant part in the city's economy during the early 20th century, as it had in the second half of the previous century; and the two main commodities which were imported here were grain and timber. Although some timber was brought in as logs, much of it arrived already sawn into 'deals' or standard lengths, which we see being unloaded by crane on this photograph. Because very large ships were not able to navigate the Severn as far as Gloucester, cargoes would be brought up from Sharpness along the canal by barge or timber 'lighter'. A significant number of timber yards grew up along the east side of the canal near the Bristol Road, and the timber trade provided many employment opportunities. There was work to be had in loading and transporting the timber; there were plenty of jobs in the wood yards and mills, of Price, Walker & Company and Nicks were once two of the largest; and there were careers for skilled craftsmen in the carpenters' and furniture-makers' shops like Lea & Company who had extensive premises along Aldate Street. Perhaps Gloucester's most famous wood factory of all was Moreland's match factory, begun by Samuel Moreland in 1868; Moreland's, makers of England's Glory matches, was taken over by Bryant & May in 1913 but the Moreland family continued to run the business, which provided employment for hundreds of local people at the Bristol Road factory, right up to 1972 - four years before the factory finally closed down.

Above: The HMV sign - with Nipper sitting beside that wonderful 'Trademark' gramophone horn, ears cocked attentively - now means rack upon rack of CDs to look through; but the sign on the left-hand side of Southgate Street takes us back to the days when long-playing records were the latest thing, offering a number of technical advantages over the old wax 78s. The really serious drawback with 78s was that they were so fragile (lovers of folk music may be reminded of Richard Thompson's song 'Don't Sit On My Jimmy Shands'), but they were also quite hard work; at 78 rpm, it didn't take long for the needle to get from beginning to end, so somebody was constantly jumping up to put the next side on. A major orchestral work could easily come in a dozen or more double-sided records; HMV's recording of Carmen comes in nineteen. And in the days of wind-up gramophones, there was also the job of cranking up between records and changing the needle after every few sides. Then came long-playing vinyl records, sapphire or diamond styli, stereophonic sound and autochange record players; if you were prepared to let your records crash down onto the turntable one on top of another you could sit back and listen to several LP sides in a row. We thought listening to Simon & Garfunkel and the Stones in stereo was mind-blowing, in spite of the scratches . . . and so we leapt from one acoustic delight to the next, through to the digital sounds of the 21st century.

Dancey + Meredith - drawing on a century of practice

Founded in 1894 by Henry A Dancey, Dancey + Meredith is now one of Gloucestershire's longest established Architectural Practices. Prior to founding his own Practice, Harry had qualified as an architect and then built up experience and expertise whilst working for a local firm, Waller & Sons. Having accrued an impressive CV with them, Harry took the bold decision to set up his own business. Thus, in 1894, the Practice that was later to become Dancey + Meredith was founded at premises in Commercial Road, Gloucester.

One of the first significant commissions for Harry was that of designing all the buildings for what was to become the Corporation of Gloucester's new electricity generating works, the power station that brought electricity to Gloucester over 100 years ago.

The buildings were built on a site of historic interest, where previously had stood part of the motte, or mound, of Gloucester's Norman castle. In order to commemorate the completion of the works Harry hosted a sumptuous banquet at the new Guildhall on 19th July 1900, along with the nine other project contractors, the chairman of the Electricity Supply Committee and the consulting engineer.

There is a memory of Harry attending a site meeting, on a horse and buggy (wearing his characteristic bowler hat) at

Above: St Margaret's Alms houses on London Road - a 13th century chapel, the refurbishment of which was completed by Dancey + Meredith in 1986.
Below: The Royal Hotel, Bruton Way (formerly The Midland and Royal Hotel), designed by Harry Dancey and completed in 1898.

son, Cyril Vinson Dancey had joined the Practice. It was Cyril, together with Roy F Meredith, who in the same year transferred premises to Bleak House, Station Road, Gloucester, where the Practice still has its base. Cyril became a licentiate of the RIBA (LRIBA) in recognition of his 20 years running the Practice, and later a fellow (FRIBA).

During the post-war years the Practice was appointed by most of the major local industrial concerns, including Dowty Rotol, Morelands Matches, Fielding & Platt, Copeland Chatterson, the Gloucester Foundry and the Babcock Group. Since then, of course, the national trend has seen a decline in industrial activity. This is reflected in the increased diversity of project types now undertaken, and the extended area of Dancey + Meredith's operation.

The Dancey family involvement in the Practice was perpetuated through the generations. In 1961 the founder's grandson, Jeremy Vinson Dancey, joined the firm. Jeremy served the family Practice for over 30 years, overseeing a period of expansion and diver-sification of project types. Sadly, Cyril Dancey died in 1971, by which time Jeremy had appointed as Partner

Quedgeley, now a major suburb of Gloucester. The journey and the meeting took him the whole day. The Practice continued to flourish throughout the subsequent years, undertaking many commissions, including city churches and hotels. It was, however, not until 1938 that the Partnership was established as Dancey + Meredith. By this time the founder's

Top: *The Morelands Match Factory, with whom Dancey + Meredith have had an association since just after the second world war. At the time of writing the firm is working on further alterations.*
Above left: *The Dick Whittington public house on Westgate Street, originally a 16th century guildhall and refurbished by the firm in 1986.*

Bob Priest. Bob had joined the Practice on leaving school in 1949. Under the direction of the new partnership the Practice continued to flourish, undertaking a wide variety of projects, many at some distance from Gloucester.

Upon Jeremy and Bob's retirement in 1993 the Practice no longer contained and Dancey family members. Despite this, the Practice continued successfully under the Dancey + Meredith name. This was made possible due to the work of Richard Cue and Neil J Dransfield. They had joined the firm in 1974 and 1975 respectively, became Associates in 1979 and then Partners in 1987. It was Richard and Neil who, in 1997, formed the present partnership and in 1998 incorporated the Company as D+M Architects Limited.

Throughout the Practice's history, Dancey + Meredith has sustained a progression of steady growth and has built up a reputation for creative yet cost effective design solutions, coupled with proven technical expertise. This reputation has contributed to the large proportion and wide variety of repeat commissions enjoyed by the Practice throughout its many years in existence. Notable amongst the clients with whom the Practice has enjoyed continuity of employment is Roadchef, for whom a large number of motorway service area and hotel developments have been constructed. The Practice also has a successful track record in the design and procurement of public houses, and is retained as Partnering Architects on a rolling programme of public house and travel inn developments for a major brewer.

The Practice has also been involved in the renovation and conversion of listed

This page: The Old Crown public house on Westgate Street. This was formerly Woods Army & Navy Stores, an 18th century building. The restoration and interior design was completed by Dancey + Meredith in 1990.

buildings and has gained a considerable number of Civic Awards as evidence of this expertise. Notable amongst such projects have been BBC Radio Gloucestershire, 'The Dick Whittington' (the restoration of a scheduled ancient monument and its conversion into a public house) and 'The Old Crown

Inn', which also won the CAMRA award for the best refurbished pub.

Over a period of some 25 years, the firm has carried out a wide variety of housing schemes on behalf of housing associations and local authorities. These schemes currently total some 1,600 dwellings and range from general family housing to sheltered flats, special needs schemes, hostel accommodation, dwellings for the disabled and refurbishment projects.

Currently the Practice continues, in its long established tradition, to be involved with a wide variety of projects, including retail parks, industrial schemes, neighbourhood centres, social housing, supermarkets, veterinary surgeries and multiplex cinemas. Reflecting the national trend, commissions now involve work around the United Kingdom, with moves towards overseas projects.

The Directors have always believed in investing in high calibre staff and have a policy of continuous reinvestment in CAD technology. The Practice operates a Total Quality Management system. These attributes, coupled with the Practice's ability to draw on more than a century of experience, enable Dancey + Meredith to remain successful into the new millennium, with a substantial order book of exciting commissions.

Left: *The offices of Dancey + Meredith on Station Road.* **Below:** *Northgate House, London Road, a 17th century building - refurbishment by Dancey + Meredith in 1983.*

Pressing ahead to build success

The company known today as Pressweld Ltd started life under the title Venesta Aluminium Products Ltd. The newly established company commenced trading in November 1963 from premises in Hanwell, West London.

It was from Hanwell that Venesta Aluminium Products Ltd began production in the fabrication and finishing of aluminium components. Almost immediately, however, it became apparent that the small Hanwell site would not be able to accommodate the demands of and up-and-coming business with plans for development and growth. As a result the company moved to Gloucester in 1964 which was to prove the ideal base and a permanent home for the growing business. The transition to Gloucester was accomplished smoothly and the company began operating from the former Gloucester Aircraft premises at Hucclecote without a break in supply and without inconvenience to customers. Initially Venesta Aluminium Products Ltd produced specialised products mainly for the domestic appliance and motor industries. These ranged from radiator grilles, headlamp bezels and fascia panels for the automotive industries to reflectors and splashback surround trims for electric and gas household cookers and fires. Indeed the company rapidly gained a highly regarded reputation for producing bright, shiny, decorative components in large quantities.

AUTOCAR—MARCH 12, 1965

VENESTA ALUMINIUM PRODUCTS LTD
To the front again!

WITH THE MOST SOPHISTICATED EXTRUDED ALUMINIUM FRONTAL GRILLE YET PRODUCED IN THIS COUNTRY

FOR THE WORLD FAMOUS STANDARD-TRIUMPH T.R.4.A

VENESTA ALUMINIUM PRODUCTS LTD
GLOUCESTER TRADING ESTATE, HUCCLECOTE, GLOUCESTER—Glos 67981

Throughout the early years of trading, Venesta Aluminium Products Ltd had not only built an enviable reputation within the industries that it served but had consequently experienced a sustained period of ever increasing business. This success meant that by the year 1967 the company was in a strong position to expand. As a result it was in this year that Venesta Aluminium Products Ltd acquired a smaller but very similar company called Pressweld. This company was based in West Molesley, Surrey and employed 20 people pressing aluminium wheel trims. The activities at the Surrey factory were restricted to power pressing only and as the wheel trims produced at Pressweld needed to be anodised before they could be sold there was a natural fit with Venesta Aluminium Products Ltd, who had recently installed a state-of-the-art anodising plant.

The acquisition of Pressweld brought about fundamental changes to the face of Venesta Aluminium Products Ltd, for not only did it enable the company to expand, it also incited a change of name to Pressweld Aluminium Ltd.

Above left: *Early advertising for the company's products.* ***Below:*** *The Hillman Super Imp, first manufactured in 1965.*

The newly expanded company could now go on to build up a business in the production of annular wheel trims. Indeed this side of the company flourished and developed a sizeable business. Classic vehicles such as the Morris Minor and the much loved Ford Cortina were fitted with Pressweld produced wheel trims and at one stage the company produced more than one million trims annually from its factories. This successful progress was set to continue and in 1973 Pressweld Aluminium Ltd was in a position to expand its factory and facilities at Hucclecote. The completion of this expansion brought with it an important turning point for the company. It was in this year that operations were consolidated from Surrey to Gloucester in order to make use of the enlarged facilities. This consolidation was also marked with a further change to the company's name, this time to its present title, Pressweld Ltd.

Throughout its history the company had been in the forefront of decorative aluminium trim manufacture with many famous names amongst its client list. Austin, Morris, Vauxhall, Ford, Triumph, Hillman, Sunbeam, Rover and Jaguar. Although today Jaguar are still a major customer, many of the other names ceased trading and consequently, during the late 1970s and early 80s, Pressweld sought other markets to replace declining motor business. These came in the form of supplying

components and assemblies for lighting units, fruit machines, gas fires, microwave and conventional cookers.

Over the following years the company continued to be a leading supplier of metal tread plates for top of the range vehicle manufacturers. Pressweld became the first company to introduce formed, one-piece extruded aluminium surround frames for built-in kitchen hob units and also the first to introduce one-piece formed and welded cabinet frames for the gaming machine industry.

The 1990s also proved to be a decade of achievement for Pressweld. Not only had the company received Pursuit of Excellence Awards from Jaguar on three occasions but in addition won Supplier of the Year from Baxi Heating in 1992. Investors in People award was gained in 1993 when the company was one of the first companies in Gloucestershire to qualify. The year 1995 was also an important one for the company as it moved to a new purpose built factory close to the historic Gloucester Docks at Spinnaker Park. The following year saw the introduction of Spraycol, a method of colour spray dyeing anodic film that even today, Pressweld are the only company in its field to offer. The 1990s ended as they began and in 1999 the company's systems and procedures were approved to QS 9000 standard - the world standard for automotive suppliers.

Today, Pressweld employs 120 people and the current Managing Director, Tony Pawson, who started with the company as a Sales Representative, believes that the future is extremely promising with excellent opportunities to supply components to European motor manufacturers as well as a very healthy domestic market.

Above left: *The Jaguar grille produced by the company.*
Top: *An exhibition from the 1990s.*

Gloucester's one-stop shop

It was perhaps inevitable that when brothers, Ken Jones and C Arthur Wicks Jones made the decision to set up in business together they would choose to open a store. Moreover, it was perhaps also inevitable that their store would be opened in Gloucester and would prove to be a successful venture.

Indeed, the brother's father himself owned and ran a successful Ironmongers store named, T J Jones and Co. Ken and Arthur both helped their father in the store and in the process, gathered knowledge and experience which was to prove invaluable to them later on in their careers.

It was not long before the ambitious brothers decided that the time had come to part company with the Ironmongers store that they had become so familiar with. They wanted to become independent from their father and so, summoned up their entrepreneurial spirit in order to set up their own business.

The brother's new business, located at Barton Street in Gloucester, was officially opened on the 8th of November, 1938 under the name, LVS (Gloucester) Limited. To some extent the store was similar to their father's in as much as they too, sold hardware items such as pots, pans and utensils. However, they also acted as wholesalers to the licensed victuallers industry and as such, supplied glassware, china, optics, cutlery, crockery, utensils, cellar equipment, and beer engines to local pubs and clubs.

With the help of their wives, Betty and Molly, Ken and Arthur's new business got off to a flourishing start. Betty and Molly did the book keeping and the general administration between them whilst Ken took care of most of the sales work and Arthur looked after the running of the office.

However, it was not long before the initial successful progress of the new business was temporarily brought to a standstill. The business was closed during the years 1940 to 1945 due to the advent of the second world war. Fortunately for the brothers, by then their business had not been operating for very long and consequently, there was not a lot to lose. Ken, who had been an RAF

Above: *Ken Jones (oval picture) and C Arthur Wicks Jones, co-founders of the company.* ***Below:*** *The family in 1919. Clockwise from top left: Tom, John (father), Arthur, Florence (mother), Nancy, Ken, Harry.*

Volunteer Reserve Pilot since 1937, was enlisted almost immediately, retrained and was soon flying Hurricanes in the Battle of Britain. Unfortunately, in 1941, he was shot down over Belgium and spent the rest of the war in different Prisoner of War camps throughout Europe. His brother, Arthur was called up in 1940 to join the Glosters. He fought in many theatres and ended the war as a Major in Burma.

It was not until 1946 that the brothers were able to resume in business when they recommenced trading in Norfolk Street, Gloucester. Despite the challenges provided by Gloucester's vales and hills for the stock vans, which often had to have their engines warmed with sump heaters before they would start, it was not long before the Jones brother's sales reps could be seen travelling around Gloucester making deliveries. Indeed, only a year later, in 1947, the brothers were able to move their shop to new premises in Southgate Street from where the company has traded ever since.

As the business developed, it was decided to expand. A new branch of the business was opened in Malmesbury in Wiltshire and later this branch was moved to Chippenham, also in Wiltshire. These branches were both successful in their own right but eventually proved to be a bad move for the business. As a result, the Chippenham branch was closed in 1979.

By 1983 the company was exceeding expectations and another branch of the business was opened in Swindon. This branch was successful for a time. However, in 1989 it was decided to close the branch and centralise distribution in Gloucester.

This decision proved to be a wise one and by 1998, the company's 60th anniversary, business was thriving. Ken's son Nick had, by then, taken over the business and remains today, the Owner and Managing Director. Indeed, Arthur's grandsons, Simon and Jim Boulton played a part in the company's history in 1999 when, with the help of their company, Evolution Commerce, they designed and installed 'pubco' - LVS (Gloucester) Limited's on-line store and web site.

Today, LVS (Gloucester) Limited continues to flourish. Indeed, with an expansive range of goods, including everything from paperware to catering equipment, the company hopes to continue to offer the licensed trade purchasers of Gloucester a one-stop-shop for many more years to come.

Above: *Harry Jones outside TJ Jones & Co in Barton Street - 1919.*
Below: *A recent exhibition.*

The perfect package of progress and success

It was in the year 1966 that the company known as Marshall Langston Limited first came into existence. The company was set up by two men, R J Langston and R J Marshall in order to design and manufacture corrugated cases and packaging.

Before establishing the business the founders had been involved in the paper industry, with RJ Langston working for the Powell Lane Manufacturing Company which had sites in both Severn Road and Commercial Road, Gloucester.

In 1966 Powell Lane, having been taken over by Reed Corrugated and moving to Lydbrook, the decision was taken by RJ Langston and RJ Marshall to set up in business together and form a new company. Consequently Marshall Langston was established.

The company started life in leasehold premises at Hempsted Bridge in Bristol Road, Gloucester. Indeed, these premises had themselves, an interesting history. Hempsted Bridge comprised of a long building which had previously been known as the

Carbide Store and before that had also, in its lifetime, been used as a salt store! From 1966 onwards however, it was to begin its life in use as the location of Marshall Langston Limited. This meant that it was now being used to produce corrugated cases and embossed paper for the biscuit and perfume markets.

The partner's new business got off to a flourishing start. However, this promising beginning was not achieved single-handedly. Both men received the help and support of their wives during the setting up and initial stages of the running of Marshall Langston Limited. R J Langston also had the good fortune of having two able and willing sons who, before joining the company full time, often came into work in order to help their father with the production of orders and other similarly useful tasks.

The first ten years of the company proved to be prosperous ones. Together, the partners watched their company steadily progress and enjoy a decade of growing success. Sadly however, the year 1978

***Below:** Marshall Langston's premises in the late 1960s.*

brought with it an end to this happy partnership. It was in this year that R J Marshall died and because he didn't have any children, all Marshall involvement in the business ceased upon his death. Despite this, although there were no Marshall's to carry on the family involvement in the company. The Marshall name remains in respect of his involvement in the company's growth.

The year following this unhappy event proved to be more optimistic. It was in 1979 that R J Langston's sons, Kevin and Neville, joined the company full time and Marshall Langston Limited became an independent family firm and continued to thrive.

Hempsted Bridge had been an ideal location for Marshall Langston in its first two decades of existence. However, it had presented several challenges along the way. The most difficult one of those being the challenge of reversing 40 foot articulated lorries across the Hempsted Lane and Bristol

Road junction into the premises. Therefore, due to the expansion and growth of the company in 1987, 21 years after first moving to the Hempsted Bridge premises, Marshall Langston moved its operations to larger, purpose built, freehold premises situated in Lower Tuffley Lane, Gloucester.

The move to the Lower Tuffley Lane premises proved to be a wise decision and the company continued in its ever increasing success. Today, with R J Langston as the company Chairman, his son Kevin in charge of Sales and Administration and Neville in charge of Production, Marshall Langston continues to produce corrugated containers made to the size and quantity that the customer wishes to purchase. Indeed, with further investment in new machinery and the help of a dedicated workforce, the company is hoping to continue as a Gloucester, independent, family owned business for many years to come.

This page: *Marshall Langston today.*

Retail therapy of ancient origin

The Gloucester City Council Markets, now situated in St Oswald's Road and Brunswick Road, are in fact, of ancient origin. It is thought that Gloucester has had the right to hold a market even before the Norman Conquest in 1066. However, it was in 1555 that the Mayor and Burgesses of Gloucester claimed that *they had been wont time out of mind to have a market every Wednesday and Saturday* with balances to weigh wool and wool-thread. Consequently, Charters were passed to this end and Gloucester saw its first weekly market.

In 1784 the City Council decided to build new markets in Eastgate Street and Southgate Street. It was intended that the Eastgate Market be used for the sale of meat whilst the Southgate Market be used for the sale of fruit and butter. The next major development was the opening of the covered Retail Market, known as the Market Hall, in Eastgate Street in 1856. Indeed, 1856 was an important year in the history of the Gloucester Markets. It was in this year that the Eastgate Market was extended and reconstructed in order to include the Southgate Market, by then known as the Corn Exchange, which was transferred there from its original location. Interestingly enough, the capital cost of the new Market was financed by the promotion of a 'tontline' by raising forty hundred pound bonds or, in other words, £4000.

It was not until the 27th October, 1958 that the new Gloucester Livestock Market, designed by the then City Architect, J V Wall, was opened on reclaimed land off St Oswald's Road, at a total of £400,000. However, this large investment proved its worth and, as one of the first completely new undertakings built in post-war years, it acted as a model for several other local authorities when planning their markets.

Before the Livestock Market could be built, the site off St Oswald's Road had to be reclaimed. The land was originally subject to flooding by the River Severn and had to be filled in up to a height of 11 feet in order to ensure that it was above the flood level. It was only then that the construction of the market facilities could begin. The 30 acre site was built to include trade offices, shops, banks, a restaurant and snack bars, open trade displays, administrative offices and extensive parking for lorries and private cars. The market consisted of a dairy section, a fat and store cattle section, a calf section, a sheep section and a pig section. Aptly, the area surrounding the market also comprised a modern public house, an abattoir and industries and showrooms with an affinity to agriculture.

The completion of the Gloucester Livestock Market proved to be a success and was followed, in 1967, with the first large comprehensive form of redevelopment ever to take place in the central shopping area of the City. After several

Above: *The front entrance to Eastgate Market.*

of the best developments of its kind in the country.

Over the following years these two major developments in the history of Gloucester City Council Markets were added to. In 1971 an Open Air Market was established in the Livestock Market and in 1999 the Eastgate Market was brightened up with a colourful mural depicting the changes in market trading throughout the ages.

Today, the Gloucester Livestock Market, the Open Retail Markets held at St Oswald's Road and

years of preparation and negotiations, the City Council entered into a partnership arrangement with Land Improvements Limited to redevelop 5.4 acres of land bounded by Southgate Street, Eastgate Street, Queen Street, Constitution Walk and Greyfriars, principally for shops, offices, an hotel, car parking and landscaped open spaces. The Market Hall became the focal point of the shopping complex and was occupied by 44 self contained, well facilitated stalls, catering for the different classes of trade. Indeed, the Eastgate Retail Market was described, at the time, as one

the Eastgate Market located at Brunswick Road still remain a thriving part of the City of Gloucester. Indeed, although the markets of Gloucester today are a far cry from those of ancient times, the claim, 'Whether it's animal, vegetable or mineral, you're sure to find it somewhere in Gloucester's Markets' is, no doubt, as true today as it was then!

Above left: *A Christmas stallholders' competition from the late 1990s.* ***Top:*** *A typical shopping day in the 1970s.*

A story of innovation and invention

Fielding and Platt Limited was founded in October 1866 by Samuel Fielding and James Platt. The partnership was initially engaged in general engineering and was based at the Atlas Iron Works in Gloucester.

James' background had been as an engineer, fitting out many West Country mills with machinery of his own design. Samuel too was an engineer but also had an outstanding business acumen and it was he who contributed the major share of capital to the partnership.

From the outset the partnership seemed destined to succeed. Indeed, the partner's first contract was booked on 12th October and its entry in the order book has 'Executed' written across it - proof of the new company's eager start!

It was not long before the company showed a leaning towards hydraulic engineering. In 1871 when Ralph Hart Tweddell presented the partners with his invention - a portable hydraulic riveter, the direction of the company was marked out for the future. From 1871 onwards the company developed and sold a variety of hydraulic machines and during the following decade obtained numerous interna-

tional awards for its contribution to applied hydraulics. Sadly, in 1874 Samuel Fielding died. However his sons, James and John Fielding, became junior partners in the business and in doing so carried on the Fielding family name.

The company experienced further success in 1882 when it designed and built a two-stroke gas engine with electrical ignition. By the year 1892 Platt and Tweddell, sometimes with John Fielding, had registered a total of 23 successful inventions! These innovative designs ensured that even after his death in 1897, the name James Platt would be preserved in the history of the company bearing his name.

The 20th century opened with two firsts for Fielding and Platt. 1902 saw the company manufacturing the first vacuum cleaner designed by the inventor, Hugh Cecil Booth - one was actually used to clean the carpet at Westminster Abbey for the Coronation of Edward VII! In 1912 the company were the first to patent the heavy oil engine which continued in production until 1939.

Above: *A group photograph of founder James Platt (left) and founder Samuel Fieldings' two sons, John and James (right).* ***Right:*** *An early vacuum cleaner produced by the company - the first to be used to clean Westminster Abbey.* ***Below:*** *A 5000 tonne Aluminium Plate Stretcher.*

The advent of the first world war saw the company manufacturing extrusion presses for the War and Ammunition Ministries. However, immediately after the war the company found its market depressed but managed to survive due to its wide range of diverse products.

1939 was a landmark year in the history of the company. It was in this year that Fielding and Platt joined forces with Heenan and Froude to form what was to become the Heenan Group. The two companies had worked together in the past, notably in 1878 during the construction of the Blackpool Tower!

During the second world war operations were again turned over to the war effort and the post war period saw the company revert to its traditional business of supplying hydraulic presses.

The 1960s opened with the introduction of automated presses. These advances inevitably aided the supply of a 5000 ton Aluminium Plate Stretcher in 1963 for the manufacture of Concorde! Indeed by 1968, two years after its 100th anniversary, the company became one of the strongest engineering groups in Britain when the Heenan Group merged with Redman Tools to form Redman Heenan International Limited.

The 1970s also began successfully. The expansion of the Gloucester site was completed in 1971; several new product ranges were introduced including a range of Deep Drawing and Ironing Presses; and the company also undertook the development, marketing and manufacture of the unique range of Redman hydraulically operated vehicle bumper-bar roll-forming machines, that continued until the advent of plastic and synthetic rubber bumpers in the late 1970s.

The company continued to operate and in 1981 Fielding and Platt achieved a major success by securing an order from Taiwan for a 4500 Tonne Aluminium Plate Stretcher.

The company underwent a management buyout in 1983 and in the following two years successfully obtained major orders from the UK and the USA. However, by 1986 the management was faced with financial difficulties and the company went into voluntary receivership. Fortuitously, the company was bought a few months later by Clayton, Son and Company (Holdings) Limited and Fielding and Platt continued to follow its markets and successfully recover some ground.

The 1990s proved to be a decade of major success and achievement for the company. In 1992 an order was secured for an 1800 Tonne Aluminium Plate Stretcher for Egypt and in 1993, another order was secured for an Aluminium Extrusion Plant for Syria. Likewise, 1995, 1997 and 1998 were all marked with major orders from the USA, the UK and Korea.

Today, Fielding & Platt International Limited, as it is now known, is part of the Material Handling Systems Division of Motherwell Bridge, the largest privately owned engineering company in the UK.

The company's business currently serves the Aerospace, Metals, Automotive and Construction industries worldwide with locations in Gloucester, Leeds and USA. Indeed, Fielding & Platt International Limited's story of innovation and invention, begun in 1866, is set to continue.

Top: *a 16MN Aluminium Extrusion Press undergoing factory test.*

Modelled on past glories

A workshop in the back garden was as good as it got when Eddie Cook, helped by his wife Peggy, set up in Gloucester in 1960 as a self-employed cabinet maker. His fine work did not go unnoticed, and he soon found himself producing, among other things, piano stools for a world famous local piano maker. He had no way of knowing, back then, that the firm he was in the process of founding would become known to antique dealers across the world - and the caption alongside a photograph of the original premises in an old album says it all: 'In the beginning it was just a crazy idea'....

Recognising the potential of the skills he possessed, Eddie branched out in other directions. Using only traditional materials such as hardwoods, reclaimed furniture, french polishes, horsehair, dyes and waxes, he took on more work restoring items of antique furniture and manufacturing fine reproductions, many of them specially commissioned - all of which led eventually to his trading in antique furniture. Among his clients at the time was Bon Marche (now Debenhams), who brought in Eddie to work on repairing their damaged stock. Even Eddie's sister-in-law, Joyce Isaacs, helped out with the upholstery and polishing. By the end of the 1960s the business in Stroud Road - by now

E J Cook and Son - was thriving, and in spite of extending the premises it was clear that before long a larger building would be needed to cope with the developing young company. The firm was rapidly gaining a reputation for excellence, and their renovation work was in demand in British Embassies throughout the world.

More staff was of course needed, and at various times Eddie was joined by his son Christopher in sales, his wife Peggy and daughter Gillian who looked after administration and accounts.

Left: Eddie Cook, who founded the company together with his wife, Peggy.
Below: Lock Warehouse before the company took it over for its new warehouse.
Bottom: Stroud Road - where it all began.

By the late 1970s the shop and workshops at Stroud Road were at bursting point, and Eddie Cook took on the biggest challenge he had yet faced - the renovation and conversion of a semi-derelict warehouse into a superior antiques centre.

Fine old furniture, china and needlework have been valued for many years - even the Victorians were avid collectors. With uncanny foresight, Jerome K Jerome anticipated the phenomenal growth in the trade more than 100 years ago in 1889: 'Will rows of our willow pattern dinner-plates be ranged above the chimney-pieces of the great in the years 2000 and odd?' he wrote, adding that '...travellers from Japan will buy up the "souvenirs of Margate"...and take them back to Jedo as ancient English curios.' How could he have known? But the fact is that at the beginning of the 21st century people across the world are more than ever attracted to antiques, curios and collecta0bles of all kinds, from Georgian mahogany kneehole desks to bakelite radios, and from Hornby Dublo train sets to 1920s Wedgwood Fairyland lustre ware - and their number is growing.

Eddie Cook did not underestimate this developing public awareness when he began the mammoth task of transforming the Lock Warehouse into five floors of memorabilia. The work was undertaken in phases, and it was a red letter day in the history of the company when the Mayor of Gloucester, Councillor Williams, declared the centre officially open on 8th December 1979.

The Antiques Centre lets space to dealers throughout the country (and to one dealer from the USA), and provides staff to sell goods on their behalf in their absence - a unique package. With space for up to 140 sellers, it proved to be an exciting project, attracting dealers to buy from the centre from as far afield as Holland, Belgium, France, the USA and Japan. Private collectors, however, are just as important to the company, as are people who simply want a day out with a difference. They go along to view the goods on offer - it is the centre's justifiable boast that they have more to see than many museums!

At the beginning of a new millennium, future plans involve giving the building a face-lift. The aims of the centre, however, are more far-reaching than mere paint and floor coverings! In a serious mission statement, the company declares its aims for the future as providing the best service at the most economic rates available, and their team of dedicated staff intend to concentrate their efforts into providing an even better service to their dealers. With such a track record of excellence, an unbroken history of success and growth, and the welfare of their dealers at the top of their priority list, the company has every likelihood of accomplishing their eventual aim - to become the Country's Number One Antiques Centre.

Above left: *The opening of the Lock Warehouse centre by His Worship the Mayor of Gloucester, Councillor Williams on 8th December 1979.* ***Top:*** *Lock Warehouse today.*

Helping to create tomorrow's traditions

In the year 1904 William John Bowles Halls, known for convenience sake as WJB, decided to found his own business. Little is known about William's formative years. However, it is known that he started his life in Birmingham during the 1800s and that whatever the circumstances of his upbringing, he grew up to be a real entrepreneur. With the aid of one Leyland lorry WJB established a haulage company in Gloucester under the name, WJB Halls Limited Haulage Contractors.

It was not long before WJB's business began to develop and expand and by July 1919 it was re-styled and officially registered as WJB Halls Limited Building Contractors.

WJB's entrepreneurial spirit meant that he had his finger in many pies. Indeed, the period between 1919 and 1950 saw WJB developing direct and financial interests in several businesses. Amongst these were two hotels in Cheltenham, two farms on the Welsh borders which were used as a frequent summer outing place for his grandchildren, the Black and White Coach Company for which he bought the first coaches and which went on to become the National Express Coach Company, the Stonehouse Brick and Tile Company from which it is said bricks were used to build the Battersea Power Station and the purchase of a number of industrial properties in Llanthony Road in Gloucester.

Despite these varied concerns WJB's main passion was for his building company. In 1905, before the company was established, houses were built on the corner of New Road, Hardwicke where land was bought for 6d per square yard and bricks cost £1 per thousand! By the 1920s however, WJB's detached houses could be picked out along the Stroud side of Gloucester due to their distinctive style. WJB himself lived in one at 215 Stroud Road and in 1935, he built number 217 as a wedding present for his daughter Elsie and her husband, Leonard Alden Keck, who lived there until 1967!

In the September of 1912, WJB purchased the land that was to become the base for his company for over 70 years. This land was situated at the corner of Barton Street and Park Road, in the area known as Barton Gates and the initial two acres were purchased from a Mrs Fanny Gurney for the total of £900! During the early days WJB rented out buildings at Barton Gate to amongst others Kell and Company and the Boy Scouts!

The building business flourished and it was not long before the company moved into contracting and began erecting buildings as far afield as Bath and Taunton. The Barton Gates

Above left: *William John Bowles Halls, founder of the company.* ***Above right:*** *A rent book from 1912.* ***Below:*** *One of the company's earliest vehicles.*

site was used for manufacturing joinery for use in the building operation and by 1935, this side of the business had grown to such an extent that the South West Joinery Company was established.

The advent of the second world war brought with it a period of change for the business. Whilst the building company continued to operate and in fact, completed the Technical College in Gloucester, the joinery company transferred its efforts into work for the War Office. Tent bottoms, dough troughs, table tops, cupboards and timber soles for Clarkes Shoes were all manufactured during the war years. Indeed, even after the cessation of hostilities work was plentiful and during the next 10 years the company was heavily involved in prefabricated buildings for housing and schools.

The 1960s proved to be a period of transition for the company. It was in this decade that, during the building of the city's swimming pool, WJB decided to take a back seat. He handed the reigns of his company over to his son-in-law, Leonard Keck and accordingly the company was renamed, Halls and Keck Limited.

Under Leonard, Halls and Keck Limited continued to thrive and in 1972, Jeremy Keck joined the company after

nine years at college and work in London. Several notable buildings were erected over the following years including the Midland Bank at The Cross which in fact, received a design award. However, in 1978, the decision was taken to concentrate efforts on the joinery manufacturing side of the business and after completing work at Gloucester Prison, the building company ceased trading but continued as a holding company.

During the following years John Willetts guided the company as its Managing Director and work was carried out at several Crest Hotels, court rooms, the Houses of Commons and Lords and just about every major museum and art gallery in London!

In 1987, the company sold its base site at Barton Gates and moved to new premises at Goodridge Avenue. The company's successful work continued and included Eurodisney in France and several court rooms including the Royal Courts of Justice.

The 1990s saw John Willetts retirement and the appointment of Chris Chaplin as managing director. Although high quality joinery destined for the contracting sector continued as the company's core business, its market base was strengthened and widened with activities in upholstery manufacture, postforming and veneering, complimenting the core activity. With its highly skilled and dedicated management and workforce the company continues to uphold its commitment of 'creating tomorrow's traditions'.

Top: *The company's premises at Barton Gates, Gloucester.*
Above left: *Wall and ceiling panelling, carving and furniture at the BBC Training Centre at Wood Norton near Evesham, hand crafted by Halls & Keck.*

Breeding success in Gloucester

The origins of the company known today as Hamilton House Group Limited, can in fact, be traced back to the year 1951. It was in this year that William Henry Turney made the decisive step which eventually led to the Group businesses of today.

It was perhaps inevitable that when Henry took the ambitious decision he would select agriculture as his chosen field. By 1951 Henry had already built up a considerable wealth of knowledge and expertise in this field and indeed, his roots were firmly established in farming. The Turney's ancestors before him had farmed on the Bedfordshire/Buckinghamshire border for generations and one of the Turney farms was actually occupied by the same family line for over 300 years! Indeed, the Hamilton family name dates back centuries and it is reputed that one ancestor was Lady Hamilton the famed companion of Lord Nelson who died at Trafalgar in 1805. This rich heritage meant that Henry was raised in an agricultural environment and by the age of 21 he had already gained enough experience on the family farm to equip him to take on a management position within the industry.

It was shortly after securing this management position that Henry decided to start developing his own low-key trading activities alongside his new role. It was in this way that what was to eventually become the Hamilton House Group Limited, first came into existence. Henry commenced the initial activities of his new business venture from Northampton. Gradually however, his efforts

Below, both pictures and facing page: *William Henry Turney pictured in the early 1950s.*

achieved a degree of success with a small but growing customer base and it was not long before Henry was able to move his fledgling business to Leicestershire and then later, on again to Berkshire.

Henry worked hard at his trade and as a result his business continued to develop over the following years. The year 1976 proved to be a landmark year in the history of the company. It was in this year that after over 25 years of dedication, William Henry Turney made the decision to hand over responsibility for his business activities. Despite this, Henry's entrepreneurial spirit would not let him sit back and rest on his laurels and he devoted his time to the task of concentrating on the management of a mere 2500 acres of land in Berkshire!

> *One of Chris Turney's first tasks was the movement of the company to Suffolk*

At this stage, Henry passed the responsibility of the business activity to his son, Chris Turney. Crucially, the business was in safe hands as, like his father before him, Chris had benefited from the Turney family history and had accrued an invaluable measure of experience within the industry. After taking the reins from his father in 1976, Chris, who is also a Chartered Surveyor, managed the business and is still doing so to this day! Under Chris' sound management the business was nurtured forward.

One of the first tasks Chris completed for the business during the mid 1970s was the temporary movement of activities to Suffolk. Indeed, it was also during this decade that the far reaching decision to diversify business activities to include property asset ownership and leisure was made.

The close of the decade, likewise, proved to be an important time for the business. It was in the year 1978 that a suitably matched location was at last found for the business and as a consequence, finally a permanent base could be established. This permanent base was located in Gloucestershire where, as the name suggests, it has been ever since! From this base in Gloucestershire, Chris Turney set about the next phase in the company's history - the establishment of an owner/occupied farm business base.

However, the development and successful progress of the family business was not all plain sailing! Although the business was lucky enough not to experience any major setbacks or problems, there were challenges along the way. In fact, it actually took some 10 years of further effort in the field of cattle breeding to get to find the right formula. Added to this was the challenge of finding the right locations for the variety of business activities. Indeed, with the leisure enterprise it took 20 years in order to identify the right location! However, the company's determination not to settle for something less than perfect became an advantage and these uncompromising high standards eventually produced the successes.

Once his core business was settled at a secure and permanent base in Gloucestershire, Chris Turney could turn his efforts to building up the farm

business base that he had already begun to establish. As such, the decade of the 1980s was productively utilised to this aim and the farm business soon flourished to new and ever increasing heights!

The initial four decades of the Turney family business proved to be years of hard graft, learning and consolidation. It was not until the 1990s that the business at last experienced a period of rapid success and growth. In the year 1995 Chris Turney, in association with his wife Jane Turney made the decision to diversify the

Above, both pictures: *Chris and Jane Turney with sons, Guy (top) and Oliver at home with their Royal Show Charolais champion 'Pen-y-parc Isobell'.*

family business even further and branch out in a completely different direction from the farm business. After a period in Partnership with Gloucester auctioneers, Bruton Knowles, Chris, in partnership with the Honourable Robert Moreton from Tortworth, founded their own firm of Chartered Surveyors at Maisemore Court by Gloucester named, Hamiltons Chartered Surveyors. This business was established specifically to specialise in looking after the interests of the agricultural community in Gloucestershire and the surrounding counties.

During 1999 the various concerns were consolidated under one umbrella - Hamilton House Group

The success of Hamiltons Chartered Surveyors was notable, and it was partly due to this smooth transition that only a short period of time later, Chris and Jane developed another subsidiary business under the name, Lady Hamilton. This grew from the overseas farm contacts into International Trading.

The year 1999 was a significantly important one in the history of the Turney family's business concerns. It was in this year that the previous years of built up experience and work really came to fruition. The several different subsidiary business concerns were all brought together and consolidated under one Group. This new Group was registered under the name Hamilton House Group Limited. The Group incorporated various other businesses alongside the existing Hamiltons Chartered Surveyors Partnership. Amongst these were Hamilton Pedigree Herds, a pedigree Charolais cattle breeding business; Hamilton House Leisure Limited; Hamilton House Estates Limited, the property management wing; Lady Hamilton Limited, the International and Retail activity wing; Hamilton Oil and the Dick Whittington Family Leisure Park Ltd.

The year 1999 also saw a major project that had been in the planning stage for over 20 years come to fruition. The project was developed under the Hamilton House Leisure Limited part of the Group, and as such was a leisure scheme which was completed with the creation of the Dick Whittington Exhibition Centre situated on the edge of the Forest of Dean. The Dick Whittington Centre is, as the name suggests, based on the life of Dick Whittington who was in fact, born in North Gloucestershire circa 1350 in the Forest of Dean District Council area. The Turney family decided to situate the Centre and Family Leisure Park on their 110 acre valley farm at Blakemore, Longhope on the edge of the Forest of Dean. The Centre was created as a tribute to the life of Dick Whittington, to his achievements and to the environment in which he lived until his death in 1423.

Amongst other attractions at the Leisure Park are a model railway, an indoor and outdoor activity centre, a pets corner, and a heritage centre. The Park is also set in an idyllic, tranquil valley where there are walks and lakes for fishing all within the atmosphere of an agricultural setting and appeals to all age groups.

Apart from these significant developments in the success of the Hamilton House Group Limited, 1999 was also a memorable year personally for the Turney family. For years in the agricultural field the ultimate goal of the Turney family was to achieve a Royal Show Championship. This goal was reached in the July of 1999 when the Turney's cow, Pen-y-Parc Isobell, became the Supreme Charolais Champion. Sadly however, five days after achieving this accolade the founder of the Turney business, William Henry Turney, died just as the Championship trophy was brought back to Gloucestershire.

Today, the Hamilton House Group Limited continues to further its success and development. Despite the increasingly diverse and expanding business concerns the Group maintains its provision of a first class service and attention to individual customer needs. The Group has come a long way since its foundation in 1951. Indeed, in 1963 William Turney had less than £100 to his name and was serving the needs of less than a dozen customers. In contrast, today, the company is moving into the status of a multi million pound company and its customer base is now in excess of 100,000!

Below: *The Dick Whittington Family Leisure Park situation west of Gloucester is projected for 100,000 visitors annually.*

A family business firmly rooted in Gloucester

The company known today as ISD Cold Stores was first established in 1947 by Edgar Moon. Before setting up his own business Edgar had been productively employed in a war time occupation working as an engineer in the aircraft industry. However, the cessation of the second world war meant that he was free to embark upon a new and enterprising business venture.

So, in 1947 Edgar successfully set up his own business in Hempsted Lane, Gloucester. With the help of his brother, Robert Moon, the new business was established under the name, Llanthony Motor Bodies. As the name suggested, the original business activity was involved in the construction of motor bodies for commercial vehicles. Indeed, one of the first jobs undertaken by Llanthony Motor Bodies was the construction of the motor body for an England Glory van owned by S J Moreland and Sons Limited!

It was not long before Llanthony Motor Bodies began to flourish. However, in the founding year of the business bad weather threatened to halt the initial success and progress of the new firm. In what have now become known as the floods of 1947, the River Severn burst its banks and flooded across the fields all the way to Hempsted Lane! Fortunately however, the floods only reached as far as a few feet away from the site of the Llanthony Motor Bodies factory and the firm's resourceful staff built a flat bottomed punt and managed to sail to work in it every day. In this way the threat from the weather was overcome and the firm was able to successfully continue in business.

The decade of the 1950s brought with it a period of change for Llanthony Motor Bodies. It was during these years that a local company, L C Mitchell, needed some aluminium panels to be stove enamelled. By this time Llanthony Motor Bodies had built up a good reputation in the area and as a result, were asked to undertake this task for L C Mitchell. Indeed, the job was successfully completed and the panels were used to refurbish some refrigerated display cabinets. However, a more far reaching result of the work was the change of direction that it initiated for Llanthony Motor Bodies.

The Gloucester firm made the decision to divert its efforts solely to the manufacture of cold rooms and

Above: *Edgar Moon, founder of the company.*
Below: *Where it all started...making motorbodies.*

refrigerated cabinets. This decision proved to be a wise one and marked an important turning point in the history of the company. Indeed, in order to reflect its change in direction, Llanthony Motor Bodies was renamed, Insulated Storage and Display.

Over the following two decades Insulated Storage and Display continued to thrive. Time was spent productively, building up the cold room and refrigerated cabinets manufacturing business, and ensuring the sustainable growth and development of the firm.

The year 1983 was an important one in the history of the company. It was in this year that the firm's founder, Edgar Moon, decided to retire from the business he had set up over thirty five years earlier. This however, was not the only major event of 1983. It was also in this year that Insulated Storage Display became part of the Westward Group and as a result, changed its name to ISD. At this time, as well as ISD, the Westward Group also consisted of Westward Refrigeration and Air Conditioning, and Russell (UK).

Only four years later, in 1987, ISD underwent another change. It was in this year, following a management buy out of Westward Refrigeration, that ISD became one of the first subsidiaries of the newly formed P & M Group Limited.

Ten years later, in 1997, the company was able to celebrate its 50th anniversary. The company moved its offices and door factory to a model industrial estate and in this same year, formed a joint venture company with a Uruguayan company in order to manufacture insulated polyurethane panels and export them to South America.

Today, as part of the P&M Group, ISD is continuing to manufacture products for most of the leading refrigeration contractors in the country. The founder's grandson, Andrew Moon is now the Managing Director of the Group and as well as carrying on the family name he continues to implement his grandfather's motto, "to be fair in all business relationships" which will, no doubt, ensure the company's continued success in the future.

Above left: *Cheese distribution centre (24,000 sq metres of insulated panels).* ***Top:*** *Hempsted Lane factory in the early 1970s.*

A driving force in Gloucester

The Gloucester company, Bennetts Coaches, was originally established in the year 1962 by Arthur Bennett. Indeed, when Arthur made the decision to set up his own business it was perhaps inevitable that he would choose to found a coach company.

Arthur Bennett had spent the initial years of his working life building up invaluable experience as a coach builder for the Gloucester Railway and Carriage Company Works. However, the company experienced difficulties which inevitably resulted in Arthur and several of his work colleagues being made redundant. This unfortunate event did in fact, eventually lead to an exciting opportunity for Arthur and indeed, was the catalyst in the foundation of Bennetts Coaches.

After being made redundant Arthur, along with several of his work colleagues, found a job at Presteel in Swindon, working as a car builder. The men needed an economical means of transport to get to work every day and so, Arthur put his ingenuity and innovation to use and came up with the idea of buying a mini-bus. It was then, in 1962, that Arthur bought his first PSV, an 11 seater Perkins engine Commer. He began transporting the men back and forth to work every day and collecting a contribution from them towards the running costs of the vehicle. It was in this way that Bennetts Coaches first came into existence.

BENNETTS COACHES, 46 GARNALLS ROAD, MATSON, GLOUCESTER. Telephone No 27850
Hire or Self Drive 9—21 Seaters.

Arthur soon found that his services were needed in the evenings and at weekends. It was not long before he began taking skittle teams and a local dance band called, 'The Unit 3' to their venues. Arthur's workload steadily increased and his daughter started helping her busy father out by keeping the company's books. Another coach company, Cathedral Coaches, gave Arthur the opportunity to take a PSV driving license with them. Arthur eagerly accepted the offer, soon passed his test and was able to drive a 53 seater coach. With the PSV license under his belt, Arthur decided to leave Presteel in order to devote all his time and energies to his new business. Indeed, he began to work full time, from his home in Garnalls Road in Matson, hiring out mini-buses for hire or self-drive.

Arthur's burgeoning business began to flourish. By 1966, the company was able to purchase its first, second hand, full size, 41 seater bus. It was also, in this productive year, that the company moved from Garnalls Road to new and improved

Above left: *Arthur Bennett, founder of the company.*
Above right: *An early advertisement.* ***Below:*** *A picture taken in 1982 of Peter, Pauline and Roy with Sheba.*

premises at the back of the Ambulance Station in Gloucester. Half an acre of land was rented from Gloucester County Council at this site and a garage and office was erected, costing £1000! From this site the company acquired more vehicles, including a 36 foot Bedford VAL14/Duple Vega Major in 1969, and also won five school contracts. Securing these contracts meant that by 1971 the company needed to extend again, this time to some rented land in Fairford.

It was during the early 1970s that Arthur's eldest son, Roy, joined the family business at the Fairford site working as a manager and mechanic. However, the operation at Fairford was closed after five years when the Council decided to run its own buses, so Roy and the coaches moved back to the site behind the Ambulance Station.

Sadly, in 1977, Arthur Bennett died. However Roy and his brother Pete, his sister Pauline and their mother, successfully took over the running of the family business. In the same year a new Ford R1114 coach was purchased and the business continued to thrive. A year later, when Glevum Coaches decided to sell up, the Bennetts expanded

the business further and bought six contracts and two coaches from them.

In 1979, the family business became Limited and P&R Bennett (coaches) Ltd was founded. A year later, the newly named company acquired more contracts from Edward's Coaches and made a successful bid for 1.1 acres of land in Eastern Avenue which it moved to in 1981. A drive-through wash was installed at the premises and the sparklingly clean coaches were guarded overnight by Sheba, an Alsatian!

The decade ended as it began and by 1987, the company owned 22 coaches and three cars and was worth in excess of £1 million! The 1990s also proved to be a decade of continuing success, development and expansion for the company. Indeed today, Bennetts Coaches undertakes school contracts, private hires and tours, park and ride schemes and continental tours. The third generation of Bennetts is now working for the company and, no doubt, will continue to ensure that the family firm remains a driving force in Gloucester for many more years to come!

Above left: The latest coach to join the fleet, a 'T' Van Hool T9. Top: The first large coach, a Bedford Harrington. Below: Eight coaches provided for local senior citizens free of charge for a day trip to Weston-Super-Mare.

Meeting the needs of Gloucester people for 800 years

The Gloucester Charities Trust, although not always known by this name, has been adapting accommodation and care to meet the needs of the people of Gloucester for 800 years!

The trust first began its charitable work when medieval monasteries were used to provide shelter for the poor and lepers. Indeed, the 'shelters' or 'hospitals' of St Margaret, St Mary Magdalen, St Kyneburgh and St Bartholomew were established around the city throughout the 12th century. By the mid 14th century, whilst retaining their monastic endowments of land, their control had passed from the church to the Burgesses of the city.

Due to the decline of leprosy during the 16th century, the 'hospitals' became more identified with the care of the infirm and elderly and in 1545, Henry VIII gave custody of St Margaret's Hospital to the Mayor and Corporation.

By the late 1800s the term, 'hospitals' gave way to 'Almshouses'. This was not the only change during this period. In 1896, the first Charity Commissioners Scheme came into being and the United Hospitals were governed as one by 18 Trustees under the new title, Gloucester Municipal Charities.

Above and below: *St Margaret's Almshouses on London Road, built in 1861.*

It was not until the 1990s that the title, The Gloucester Charities Trust, was adopted and a variety of extra care facilities were added, including Magdalen House Nursing Home, Kimbrose Day Centre, both at St Margaret's, and Guild House Residential Home in Denmark Road.

Today, the trust is able to accommodate 200 people, provide Day Care for a further 100 people from the wider community and employ 140 staff. The Trust's area of benefit was extended by the Charity Commissioners to include the whole of the County and the Trust now offers the complete spectrum of accommodation and care for the elderly, short of hospitalisation. Indeed, the Trust is perhaps more in tune with the times than ever before and as such, is set to continue providing care for the people of Gloucester for many more years to come.

By the mid 20th century the Charity had reduced in size to operate from just one site, St Margaret's, where the replacement almshouses of 1861 still stand today alongside the 13th century St Margaret's Chapel. Since 1977 the charity has expanded and four new buildings of sheltered flats have been erected, including St Margaret's, St Bartholomew's, St Mark's Court and St Philip's Court. Indeed today, the number of sheltered flats stands at 130!

Above left: *St Margaret's Chapel, dating from the 14th century, still in use by the Trust today.* ***Top:*** *HRH The Duchess of Gloucester opening KimbroseDay Care Centre in 1997.*

Coleford families wending their way to Church for the annual Harvest Festival celebrations.

Acknowledgments

We are pleased to acknowledge help from the following:

The Gloucester Citizen for permission to reproduce photographs from their archive. Mr Bev Ward, Mr John Lovell and Mrs Madeline Bourne of The Gloucester Citizen.

Mr Graham Baker, Reference and Local Studies Librarian, Gloucester Central Library.

Mr Bob Light and Mr Bill Cole of Cheltenham.

Mrs Judith Taylor and Gloucester WRVS.

Our grateful thanks are also due to Andrew Houldey who edited the book.

Thanks are also due to Margaret Wakefield who penned the editorial text and Ann Ramsdale for her copywriting skills